THE CRAFT OF
WRITING POETRY

Other Allison & Busby Writers' Guides

How to Write Stories for Magazines by Donna Baker
How to Write Five-Minute Features by Alison Chisholm
A Practical Poetry Course by Alison Chisholm
How to Write for the Religious Markets by Brenda Courtie
How to Produce a Play by Doris M. Day
The Craft of Novel-Writing by Dianne Doubtfire
Writing for Radio by Colin Haydn Evans
How to Publish Your Poetry by Peter Finch
How to Publish Yourself by Peter Finch
How to Write a Play by Dilys Gater
The Craft of TV Copywriting by John Harding
How to Write A Blockbuster by Sarah Harrison
How to Write for Children by Tessa Krailing
How to Write Crime Novels by Isobel Lambot
The Craft of Food and Cookery Writing by Janet Laurence
Dear Author . . . by Michael Legat
How to Write Historical Novels by Michael Legat
Writing Step by Step by Jean Saunders
The Craft of Writing Romance by Jean Saunders
How to Create Fictional Characters by Jean Saunders
How to Research Your Novel by Jean Saunders
How to Write Realistic Dialogue by Jean Saunders
How to Write Advertising Features by John Paxton Sheriff
The Craft of Writing TV Comedy by Lew Schwarz
How to Write Science Fiction by Bob Shaw
How to Write and Sell Travel Articles by Cathy Smith
How to Compile and Sell Crosswords and Other Puzzles
   by Graham R Stevenson
The Craft of Writing Articles by Gordon Wells
The Magazine Writer's Handbook 1997/8 by Gordon Wells
The Book Writer's Handbook 1996/7 by Gordon Wells
How to Write Non-Fiction Books by Gordon Wells
Writers' Questions Answered by Gordon Wells
Photography for Article-Writers by Gordon Wells
The Best of Writers' Monthly by Gordon Wells
How to Write and Sell a Synopsis by Stella Whitelaw
How to Write for Teenagers by David Silwyn Williams
How to Write and Sell Interviews by Sally-Jayne Wright

THE CRAFT OF WRITING POETRY

Alison Chisholm

a&b

This edition published in Great Britain in 1997 by
Allison & Busby Ltd
114 New Cavendish Street
London W1M 7FD

First published in Great Britain in 1992 by Allison & Busby

Reprinted 2001

A catalogue record for this book is available from
the British Library

ISBN 0 74900 289 1

Printed and bound in Spain by
Liberduplex S.L., Barcelona.

CONTENTS

1 WHY WRITE POETRY?   1
Concerning poets. The craft. Preparation.
Thoughts to retain.

2 THE FIRST SPARK   8
Finding the idea. Nurturing the idea. Imagery.
Exercises.

3 CHOOSING THE WORDS   19
Problem words. New ways with words. Word
sounds. Punctuation and grammar. Exercises.

4 RHYTHM AND METRE   28
Metre. Iambic metre. Introducing variety.
Other metres. Different feet. Exercises.

5 RHYME   38
Full rhyme. Slant rhyme. Syllabics. Unrhymed
verse. Exercises.

6 FORM   46
Some well-known forms. (Couplets. Quatrains.
Ballad Stanza. Kyrielle. Rubai. Pantoum. Triolet.
Chaucerian Roundel. Rondel. Rondeau. Terza
Rima. Villanelle. Petrarchan Sonnet.
Shakespearian Sonnet. Limerick.) Syllable count
forms. (Cinquain. Haiku. Clogyrnach.)
Calligramme and concrete. Exercises.

7 WHILE YOU WRITE . . .   63
Finding a form. Subject material. Are you sitting
comfortably? The first draft. Fixing the mind.
Enjoy the writing. The title. Pitfalls. Exercises.

8 REVISION   73

Listening to the words. The detailed analysis.
(Overall effect. The pattern. Line structure. Rhyme,
rhythm and metre. Word choice.) The whole poem.
Your first reader. The final stages. Exercises.

9 TWO POEMS – START TO FINISH   81

Free verse poem. (Initial idea. First draft. Revision.
Third draft. Final stage.) Set form poem. (Initial
idea. First draft. Revision. Criticism. Second draft.)
Exercises.

10 PUBLICATION   99

Little magazines. Preparing poems for submission.
Collections. Other outlets. Getting organised.
Exercises.

11 THE WORLD OUTSIDE   110

Compete. Communicate. Circulate. Congregate.
Write on.

USEFUL ADDRESSES   119

1

WHY WRITE POETRY?

According to Shelley, a poem is 'the very image of life expressed in its eternal truth'. Wordsworth defined poetry as 'the spontaneous overflow of powerful feelings; it takes its origin from emotion recollected in tranquillity'. Thomas Hardy speaks of 'emotion put into measure', and Edgar Allan Poe of 'the rhythmical creation of beauty in words'.

There are as many definitions of poetry as there are readers and writers of it. Each of us has our own perception of the subject based on personal experience.

For me, writing a poem is a way of coming to terms with the world around me and the universe within me. It is an exhilarating and exhausting task. It makes sense of existence.

From the earliest times, poetry has been a part of man's way of life. Before words could be written down, culture, history, folk lore and stories were passed on by word of mouth, and the bard who carried this information in his mind was an important and respected member of the community.

With the recording of language came the opportunity for poetry to develop out of these early roots and to encompass ever-widening fields of experience.

There are no logical reasons for writing poetry. After all, the world would not stop rotating if nobody ever produced another poem. The human race would not be wiped out if all poetry books were removed from the shelves. And yet for those of us who have no choice but to write it, a world without poetry would be too appalling to contemplate.

Writing poetry means embarking on a lifestyle of hard and demanding work for little fame and less reward. Writers of prose may look forward to a bestselling novel or a West End hit. The poet labours for publication in small-circulation magazines offering payment of a few pounds and a free copy, or a slim volume destined to gather dust on the deepest shelves of his local bookshop. And yet the poet continues to write out of a driving compulsion to communicate his thoughts. (I shall refer to the poet as 'he' for the sake of convenience, but this invariably means 'he or she'.)

You do not need any qualifications to be a poet. The urge to communicate is enough. This is a mixed blessing. It leads to an assumption that anyone who can put words on to paper can write poems. It also leads many writers to believe that the words they have poured on to paper are sacrosanct, and have an automatic entity as poems. Fair enough – as long as the work produced is written for the pleasure of its creator, with no thought of publication.

All too often these outpourings are bad or at best mediocre poems. Writing good or even adequate poetry takes practice and infinite care. At the end of writing, you may even feel weak and drained, just as you do after a dose of 'flu.

There are no absolutes in poetry, so terms such as 'good' and 'bad' must be subjective. Some people feel it is unfair to judge poetry and that it should be allowed to stand immune to criticism. I think that this is a mistake. If there is no criticism, there is no need to strive. As we each set our own criteria of quality, there is no limit to the number of poems in the running for the title of 'best piece created'. When emotional response is considered alongside perceptions of quality, our favourite pieces will range boundlessly through the whole spectrum of written work.

For me, 'bad' poetry is sloppily written, lacking structure, a tired rehashing of ideas in an unoriginal way. It shows scant respect for the language and culture of which it is a part.

'Good' poetry makes precise use of language and technique, has the ability to excite and surprise, offers new insights, opens unimagined windows in the mind. It can be enjoyed afresh every time it is read. It should be constructed from the best writing you are capable of producing.

Poetry should always make its presence felt. This does not mean that every phrase must be heavy with political or philosophical theories. There is room for levity, humour and joy. There is a place for the poem which is comfortable to read, which is undemanding and does not disturb. But even a brief lyric on a slight subject should possess the indefinable magic quality that makes its reader respond. The poem which inspires no reaction at all is one which disappoints immeasurably.

You should write with total fidelity. This does not restrict you to writing only in moments of inspiration. It means that you should always write the truth as you see it, remaining faithful to your own imagination and experience, and while writing should be completely immersed in the poem.

From the moment of starting to write, you should be aware of the place of your poem within the total spectrum of poetry produced. This awareness does not imply that every line set down is destined for immortality. Instead it instils a sense of place and occasion. You write your poem in the full knowledge that it is representative of the period and style in which it was written, and if it is recorded, it stands through the future as a monument to that.

Such a global stance may feel ridiculous to the individual. It helps if you consider not just yourself, but the whole range of poets engaged in their craft.

Concerning poets

So who is producing poetry nowadays? There is no such thing as a typical poet. Indeed, many writers are reluctant to apply the term 'poet' to themselves, believing that it is some sort of honour to be conferred by future generations. I prefer to think of anyone actively writing poetry as a poet, in the way that a person who teaches is a teacher, or one who lays bricks is a bricklayer.

Poets come from all walks of life and educational backgrounds. They come from every culture in the world, every creed and colour, both sexes. They may be of any age, working or not, loners or sociable, healthy or ailing. They may be determined to see their writing in print, or interested only in setting poems down for their own satisfaction, without thought of publication.

The one thing they have in common is a love of words, a fascination with language and a delight in manipulating it. Poets are the people who can never look up a word in a dictionary in less than ten minutes, because they are intrigued by the other words

3

on the page and have to stop to read them all. They enjoy word games, crosswords, anagrams, Scrabble, puns and riddles.

Poets are keen observers, and bring a special sensitivity to their observations. It is impossible to say whether they experience life more keenly than anyone else, but they feel as though they do.

Unfortunately sensitivity and love of words are not in themselves enough. There is a lot of groundwork to cover if you want to write to the best of your ability. Just as an interest in cars and possession of a socket set will not make you a motor mechanic, so an interest in poetry and possession of a ballpoint pen will not make you a poet.

The craft

If you aim to write as well as you possibly can, you should never underestimate the value of studying the craft of poetry. Such study is more important than a flow of ideas or a flood of inspiration. It is a wonderful experience when a poem presents itself to you in finished form, or when an idea burns to be written. But it is also a rare experience, and cannot be relied upon to satisfy the urge that compels you to create poetry.

By concentrating on the craft of writing you are doing two things. You are building up a solid collection of work, remembering that no piece of writing is ever wasted effort. The experience you gain from producing it is invaluable. At the same time you are practising techniques of writing in order to make them part of your own creative process. So when inspiration strikes you have the means to deal with it at your fingertips; you do not dissipate creative energy working out the rhyme pattern for a particular form, or wondering where the line breaks should come in a piece of free verse.

There comes a time, possibly within every poem you write, when you have to step back from your study of craft and let instinct take over. Perhaps this instinct, abstract and ethereal, is the part of you which adds the touch of mystery to poetry and moves it beyond the ordinary.

I do not know whether the potential for instinct is present in all of us. If you love words, you probably possess the potential, and will develop it further with every poem you read and with every poem you write.

A serious interest in poetry involves the investment of a lifetime. You have to persevere, to continue producing more and more work, and the interest you draw is the enhancement of your life, a richness you might never have dreamed.

A passing interest in poetry will be less demanding, but will be a source of joy for as long as you wish.

This book sets out to look at the ingredients you need to make a poem. Although language, form, imagery and so on have to be considered separately, you should never forget that they must all work together for the poem to achieve its effect.

There is no virtue in producing a poem with accurate rhymes if the vocabulary makes nonsense of the piece. The most cleverly sustained image will not support a poem whose rhythm falls apart. But by studying the ingredients of a poem individually, you gain the ability to pinpoint problem areas within a piece and to correct them in order to strengthen the poem as a whole.

Each generation of writers has an advantage over every generation that went before, in that there is a larger store of work produced in the past to buttress that written in the present. In practical terms, there is an ever-increasing stock of blueprints for writers in the form of all the poems ever recorded. We can look at them to discover what is effective and what is not; which rhyme schemes flow naturally and which feel awkward; whether the shape of the printed poem can alter our interpretation of it; which subject matter occurs most frequently.

We play our own part by adding the poetry of today to this stock for the benefit of the poets of tomorrow.

Preparation

A large part of the preparation needed for you to write poetry has already been done. It consists of building up a lifetime's experience. The stockpile is there now, and will be supplemented with every day that passes.

You do not have to go through exciting adventures or great

5

traumas to produce this store. Everything you perceive with any of your senses or emotions adds to it. Look at the world with the poet's mind. Its despairs and its wonders are your source material.

Poetry is created out of an amalgam of life experience and imagination. Allow imagination to furnish the circumstances about which you want to write. Experience will supply the sensations and reactions to flesh out the writing. By transferring the emotional reactions from your store into the circumstances of the poem, you will be writing with fidelity even if your subject matter involves something you have never actually experienced.

Be willing not just to explore your thoughts, but to delve into them until it hurts in order to establish a core of truth.

Keep your outlook on life fresh. Question constantly, just as a small child does. See the world through a child's eyes and you see it with simplicity. This clarity of vision should remain throughout your writing, while the poet's craft is being grafted onto the child's observation.

Keep an open mind, so that you can explore every idea from all possible angles. You may surprise yourself with sudden insights and discover thoughts which cast a new interpretation on preconceptions.

Allow no bounds to limit your imagination. Let yourself consider wider and ever more preposterous theories. By doing so you will both clarify your vision and add an extra dimension to your writing.

Read the poetry of others. Read widely, in all styles, contemporary work and the poems of the past. Read pieces from different cultures and different languages – in the original if possible, in translation if not. Assimilate as many styles of writing and approaches to poetry as you can.

Some writers worry that by expanding their knowledge of the work of others they are running the risk of unintentionally plagiarising this work. It is more likely that their own pieces will gain depth from a fuller understanding of poetry.

Thoughts to retain

The poet is as much a craftsman as an ideas person. While all the skill in the world will not compensate for a total lack of imagi-

6

nation, brilliant thoughts will lose their impact if they are handled inadequately.

Poets do not have to be born to the task. It needs only the slightest spark of imagination to ignite a fire of talent. The spark is coaxed by a willingness to study and learn.

We should not lose sight of the fact that we are learning constantly. Writing we have produced in the past may be improved by alteration as we discover new techniques and consider fresh ideas. But bear in mind that it is natural and desirable for writing to change, going through a series of developments as our experience deepens. Returning to the work of the past to effect improvements should be done with care. It is all too easy to iron out the spontaneity of earlier writing by imposing on it techniques discovered later on.

It is as useful to explore ways of breaking the 'rules' of poetic technique as it is to learn them in the first place. Study and practise them thoroughly in order to break them effectively.

It is an unusual writer who never experiences fallow periods devoid of ideas. Be assured that these phases are not as empty as they might seem. You may feel frustrated, even agonised. But this is all part of the process of poetry. Areas of your mind are still writing, even though you may not be aware of them. Try not to panic, but wait for the flow to start again. Do not be surprised if the flow is replaced by a flood.

Remember that you are not always aware of just how much is going into a poem as you write it. It is not unusual for readers to discover depths you did not know were there or even for you to find them yourself on rereading your work. This is part of the joy of poetry, and another aspect of its magic. An apparently simple piece can open up vistas of ideas that excite and stimulate. They are not imposed by the writer, but speak naturally from the page to the reader's mind.

Finally, remember that nothing in this world compares with the wonderful feeling you get when you have written a poem that pleases you. This afterglow of satisfaction transcends thoughts of profit or fame. It is the greatest possible reward for the sheer labour of creating poetry.

2

THE FIRST SPARK

There are poets who never have to wonder where the next poem will come from. Their brains teem with inspired ideas. Ask them where they find these ideas and they will tell you they do not have to look. The air is thick with them, and the problem is choosing which to use first.

If you are never short of ideas for poems, you are a most fortunate writer. While everyone longs to be presented with the germ of a poem which will move mountains, it is not unusual to end up gazing at a blank piece of paper and planning to take up something far more creative, such as knitting dishcloths.

The trouble is that the dedicated poet has an urge, an almost physical need to write poetry. He will only feel fulfilled when his writing is flowing from the pen.

In this the poet is no different from any other writer. The difference is in the surge of creative energy needed to spark the piece to life before words can be set on to paper. Even the slimmest of slim volumes of poetry represents a huge input of initial thrust.

Those people writing longer works have an advantage. Novelists or playwrights need to find this initial spark just once at the start of each book or play. On every subsequent occasion when sitting down to write they have characters and events on which to build. They can channel all their creative forces into advancing the plot and developing the characters rather than dissipating these forces in the search for a theme.

As a poet you should be aware of the need to keep your eyes and mind open all the time for suitable material. Even the slightest hint of an idea should be written down in the notebook that never leaves your person. Snippets of conversation, a turn in the weather, a whim or daydream, a snail crossing the road are all notebook worthy. Every unusual phrase or minute description should be recorded.

As an example of note recording, here are some phrases from my notebook, and later in this chapter I shall show how they came to be translated into a poem. After a visit to Hexham Abbey I wrote:

> Steps in Hexham Abbey. Stone worn thin.
> Chart of names.
> The longevity of sanctity.
> Cold.

Remember that if these things are not written down at once they will disappear into the ether. Your sense of loss is enormous when you realise you have forgotten some little gem. However unprepossessing it might have seemed at the time, its very elusiveness adds weight to the loss. You can waste a lot of time agonising over the elusive lost phrase; so be sure it is harnessed to the memory by means of words on paper.

There will be occasions when ideas simply will not present themselves to you, no matter how great is your need to be writing poetry. When this happens, you can resort to games or exercises in order to stimulate the imagination. A list of these appears in the next section, and you will almost certainly be able to think of more suggestions of your own to add to the list.

This business of 'tricking' the mind into working on a particular theme may seem calculating and not at all artistic. It need not be so. For you are only looking for the tiniest thread of an idea when you practise this. By the time you have employed all the craftsmanship that shapes the final poem, the way you came by the idea will be forgotten or at least totally insignificant. You will have taken the suggestion on board and worked on it until any lack of spontaneity in its evolution is irrelevant.

Finding the idea

Here are fourteen sources of ideas for those frustrating times when you know you have to write something and the brain goes numb. They can be used over and over again, producing original work on each occasion.

1. Tap into your memory store. Recall not just the events of the memory, but your own reactions to them and all the sensations you experienced. The memory may be remote or recent.

2. Recall a dream you have had. Remind yourself of its story and explore the feelings you experienced while you were dreaming and when you woke up. (Day-dreams may also be used to good effect.)

3. A moment of truth. Think about your reactions to one of those startling moments when you feel in tune with the universe around you. Explore those reactions in poetry.

4. An emotional experience. Use the emotions you encountered when you fell in love, were bereaved, had a shock. You will not necessarily write about that experience, but rather use the emotions connected with it to produce a poem on a different subject.

5. Read poetry – the poetry of others, in all styles and on all subjects. Do this, not in order to produce a pale imitation of somebody else's work, but to stimulate your thoughts into the channels and rhythms of poetry.

6. Select a word at random, by sticking a pin into a page of print if you like, and produce a 'stream of consciousness' writing around the word. Just put down all the thoughts that occur to you, words or phrases, in any order, however close to or distant from the original word they appear to be. Set yourself a strict time limit of, say, two minutes. Analyse the direction your thoughts have taken. There may be a poem hidden away on the page. (An example of this exercise appears in Chapter 9.)

7. Take two entirely different subjects and see if you can weave them together through a series of parallels. For example, think about a duck and a feeling of loneliness. Draw parallels by seeing the duck swimming alone against the flow of the river. Imagine a person swimming alone, or standing alone. Read his

mind and discover the reasons for his loneliness. Refer back to the duck by focussing on water imagery throughout the emerging poem.

8. Explore *objets trouvés*. Examine the little treasures or unexpected trifles you find about the house. Hold and feel them, noting their size, smell and texture. They may offer an idea for a poem.

9. Borrow the title of somebody else's poem, painting, musical composition or work of literature. See what emerges when you present yourself with that same title. Make the poem your own by rejecting the 'borrowed' title and finding an original one.

10. Write from pictures. Use a picture on your wall, a photograph or postcard, or a picture from a book. Examine it minutely, noting the route your eye takes through the picture, the effect of light and shade, the atmosphere created. Does it intrigue or disturb you? If so, there may be a poem to come.

11. Explore a historical, legendary or fictional event through the eyes of an onlooker or participant. Try putting forward the serpent's point of view in the Garden of Eden, Mr Rochester's emotion when he first sees Jane Eyre, an ordinary sailor's reaction to the death of Nelson.

12. Present yourself with a frame, and write a detailed account of what you see in it and how you react to your observations. Your frame could be a large window or a square inch of your living-room wall. You may write factually, or allow your imagination to run wild.

13. Write something topical. Let any item in the day's news prompt you to produce a poem, being aware that strong reactions to a true story can blur your judgement of the quality of your writing. It is particularly important to stand at a distance from a topical poem and force yourself to be critical of your work.

14. Tell yourself you will not be writing an actual poem, but that you are going to spend a few minutes thinking up ideas. Make notes for at least five ideas you would like to explore in the future. If one of them prompts you to start writing immediately, well and good. If not, you have the list for future consideration.

Nurturing the idea

Important as it is to get something down on paper, it is also essential to allow the idea to mature in your mind. Let it lie there for a while, tossed about with the more humdrum concerns of everyday life, gaining strength and vigour as it grows.

The initial idea does not have to be world shattering. It may be quite a simple observation. It may be uninspiring, or downright unpleasant. Do not reject it. Give it the opportunity to prove its worth. It may leap up and surprise you.

When the idea has had a chance to settle, tune into your subconscious and let it work for you. Dredge the idea into the front of your thinking and see what is sticking to it. Other thoughts which seem, on the surface, to have nothing to do with the central idea may accompany it. Ask yourself why. Examine the relationship between the idea and its adherents. Store the results. They may well present useful material to buttress the central thought.

The Hexham Abbey idea emerged with a fragment from a Bible story clinging to it. The flight of stone steps was linked with Jacob's dream of a ladder climbed by angels, and some time afterward, that flight of steps was the part I remembered most clearly. The word 'cold' was recorded, but my January visit had been warmed by central heating. I found myself sympathising with the faithful who had worshipped there in the bitter cold of a northeast winter, and recalled the physical pain of breathing very cold air into the lungs. I remembered how the chart of incumbents bore some single names, from the days before identification was by forename and surname. These ideas went back into storage along with the original notes, reading:

Ladder climbed by angels – path to follow?
Pain of breathing, labouring for breath. Skin icy.
Names predating surnames.

As your idea emerges, examine it from all angles. First, ask yourself whether it is original. The chances are the answer will be no. There are not many ideas around which have total freshness. It has all been said before and, to be realistic, probably said more stylishly by somebody else.

This in itself should not deter you from using the idea. For however many people have offered their treatment of your theme in the past, nobody has yet viewed the subject through your eyes, bringing your unique experience to bear on it. If your treatment can be totally honest to your interpretation of the subject, your uniqueness will be inherent in it.

For example, most people would accept that Wordsworth's poetic exploration of daffodils is interesting and readable. If you wrote a poem about daffodils it would be no less valid than Wordsworth's, provided that your poem furnished your view of and reactions to the flower. Give a pale imitation of the master's work, and your piece will be forgotten.

As you consider your idea, think carefully about the best viewpoint from which to express your thoughts. To return to the daffodil example, you could write from the point of view of an observer who sees daffodils, or the daffodil itself, or somebody thinking about daffodils, or an inanimate object in the scene, such as a rock.

It is a good experiment to sit down and explore the possibilities of writing from each of these angles, and any more that occur to you. You might be surprised to note the strength given to a subject by an unexpected viewpoint. You might find your original standpoint was the right one. Do not worry. The time spent experimenting on different angles is never time wasted. It is part of the apprenticeship to the craft of poetry from which the true poet never graduates.

While playing with the idea, you may well come to realise that it was not the inspired suggestion you at first thought. The idea may be too slight to make a poem but may still have its place as one strand of another poem.

Ideas which come to you in the night and seem to be flashes of brilliance may seem dull and overworked by day. An idea may even be too complex for the poem you want to write. It may fit more comfortably into the form of a short story or even a novel. If this is the case, try writing the poem whether or not you feel it will work, and then give your idea a treatment in another form.

After writing your short story or whatever, go back to your notebook and make another attempt to express your idea in the form of poetry. You may well be surprised by the second poem you produce. Writing the idea out in a different form is a wonderful way of clearing the mind and bringing disparate images into focus. And you have a bonus in the additional piece of writing you have added to your collection.

Sometimes you will find that the more you think about an idea, the harder it becomes to know where to start in the business of selecting material and putting it in order. One possible solution is to put all your material aside for a while. Return to it a few days or weeks later with a fresh outlook. If you decide to persevere with it straight away, you may find it useful to make a list of all the thoughts that flit through your mind in connection with the idea. Some will have grown with it and others will have occurred out of the blue while you were putting pen to paper. Write each thought on a new line. Resist the temptation to keep reading over the list. Just keep writing until your thoughts have been exhausted.

When you come to read through the work you will probably find all sorts of repetitions. Do not score them out immediately. The fact that they are repeated may become an important facet of the poem. Analyse the list of notes with a highlighter pen, marking the passages which seem most useful for the poem you are going to write. Do not on any account throw the rest away. Keep the original list. It will serve as further source material throughout the writing of that poem, and may well have some overflow material which will fuel your next.

This selection process often shows the direction of the emerging poem. Do not be alarmed if your writing is going off at a tangent to the central idea. While your thoughts continue to flow, let them take you where they will. There is time enough afterwards for cutting and reshaping. Now is the moment to allow creativity its head, and perhaps to produce something totally unexpected and shining with its own truth.

By following a new course with a poem, you are not abandoning your original thoughts about its direction. They are still there for you to use on another day in another fashion, and should be treasured for such future use. Just be thankful once again for the bonus of an extra piece that is emerging.

Imagery

From the moment the idea for the poem is conceived, you should be aware of the rush of imagery that will infiltrate and support it. Images create a series of sensory perceptions in the reader, and work most strongly when they are unforced and appear to rise effortlessly from the page.

Chapter 1 referred to poetry being written out of a combination of your imagination and life experience. Running through your entire poetry output there will be messages, open or hidden, prompted by your unique self.

Similarly the reader brings his own combination of imagination and experience to the interpretation of the poem. No two readers will view a poem in the same way. Each will find his reading coloured by his own observations.

For example, you may write a poem about a glorious summer day from your childhood, where the image of eating an ice cream signifies a thoroughly enjoyable time. A reader who is allergic to ice cream will pick up bad vibrations from this image, for reasons he may not be able to identify. He will find the poem disturbing and contradictory.

This is not a problem. Divergence of opinion shows the poem's strength in its ability to stir up different reactions. And the poem only begins to work when its reader gains some sort of stimulus or feedback from it.

While constructing the poem, you should be aware of the steady build-up of images from the beginning. Do not forget that they stimulate each of the senses and also imply all sorts of emotions.

Going back to the ice-cream image, the senses of sight, smell, taste and touch are indicated at once. But think of the emotions that can be aroused by the picture of a single ice cream dropped at the water's edge; of the parent holding two ices and desperately seeking the lost child for whom one was intended; of the sheer sensuality of two lovers sharing a single cone. So a simple image may be used to convey a wide range of nuances of meaning.

It is up to you as the writer to decide which pictures within a scene will be selected for special mention. While a photograph of a wood could include trees, undergrowth, grass, paths, sky, clouds and flowers, a poem about the same scene might not mention the trees at all, but focus on the dimness of filtered light. It might say nothing of flowers or undergrowth, but describe the winding route of the path, and so on.

Through this selection you can heighten the experience of the wood for your reader, dwelling on its hostile quality, or its welcoming aspects, or the depth of its secret places. At the same time you can allow him to make the poem intensely personal by furnishing it with a wood out of his own memory.

In returning to the basic idea of the Hexham Abbey poem, I decided that I did not want to offer the reader a guided tour of the place. Rather, I wanted to pick out certain features for comment, hoping that they could both sum up my feelings about my visit and remind others of similar churches they might have seen. I chose the steps and the board of names to highlight the particular abbey, and made further notes:

> Steps taken to worship. A dream of angels.
> Footprints of saints and holy men.
> Single names.

The cold, the stone monuments and the sound of an organ were representative of Hexham, and yet would set up, I felt, a chain of images in the mind of any reader who had ever been to an ancient church. I added:

> Air like rock. Labour.
> Organ soaring. Rafters soaring.

16

Altar and paving stones concealing human remains.

These brief notes were the only ones I made before putting pen to paper to write the poem. All of the notes were incorporated in the final piece, which was first published in *Orbis* magazine in this form:

Hexham Abbey

This was no ladder for a dream of angels.
Stone steps hold footprints
of saints and holy men.
Air chilled to hard rock
laboured their lungs,
skin flinched at touching.
Those were days a single name
identified, and monuments
were tangible. Bone filled altar,
relics for carpet, cold sarcophagi
bear witness to a faith
whose sanctity is soaring rafters,
roar of organ, praise in glass.
The pictures fade into an overview
of abbeys visited across the years;
and yet that flight is fixed,
a staircase in the mind,
a route for following.

It is possible to build up a whole range of images working on different levels in the same poem, thanks largely to the richness of our language and the subtleties of definition between one work and another.

For example, imagine a love poem written from the point of view of a man who observes his lover reading a book. This is a clear picture with which we can all identify. Now consider the poet's options. He could present a picture of a woman absorbed in the reading, and ignoring the man who watches her; or she could offer to share the story with him; or she could be reading absent-mindedly, her thoughts apparently elsewhere. She could be sitting with the book on her knee, lounging full length and poring over it, flicking through the pages. Each of these implies a different insight into the situation being represented.

On another level there are overtones connected with book reading. We may infer escapism, learning or sheer enjoyment from the idea of reading. Our own love or dislike of books will colour the effect of the poem.

The word 'book' has an additional meaning, in the sense of to save or reserve. This offers a subtle hint about possession. 'Reading' implies coming to terms with a situation as well as scanning words on a page.

When you are engaged in writing the poem, such subtleties do not normally enter into your thoughts. When you revise the poem you are more likely to notice them and be aware of their implications. So this delicate underpinning of your writing is a form of serendipity which relies on your fidelity to the images you are creating.

Exercises

1   Go back to the list of fourteen ways to find ideas. Try the first of these, not attempting to produce a poem but writing detailed notes. Put the notes away and do not look at them for a week. Take them out again, and see whether you wish to alter or modify them in any way. You may have good material for a poem now, or you may put the altered version away for consideration in the future.

2   Have another look at the 'Hexham Abbey' poem. Make a list of the thoughts that occur to you in response to the images there. Expand on these thoughts from your own experience and make notes for a poem on the subject of a particular ancient building you have visited.

3

CHOOSING THE WORDS

From an early stage in the writing process, perhaps as soon as you start putting your poem down on paper, it is important to think carefully about the tone of your vocabulary. All writers need to use the language with precision. For the poet this is particularly important. Poetry is the most sparsely worded form of writing, and because it is so compact the reader's eye rests on each word. You cannot skim through a poem in the way you can skim through a story, or much of the meaning will be lost. One word which does not quite fit into its context mars the whole piece.

For the same reason overused words and hackneyed expressions draw attention to themselves and should be avoided unless you are using them deliberately in order to make a point.

Do not be afraid of speaking with your own voice through your poetry. There is no need to use flowery language that does not come naturally. Plain words express your meaning more eloquently than a jumble of vague euphemisms.

Remember that your voice will undergo subtle changes as you write. Just as we use a different tone when speaking to small children, to an employer, to a close friend, on the telephone, so our writing adopts a fresh nuance of tone to suit each poem. The overall voice is the same, but the tonal shading is varied.

The conversational feel of free verse might be out of place in strict form poetry, where a heightened effect is required. Similarly the direct style of a narrative poem would detract from the musical quality of a lyric.

By reading aloud the poetry of others and by listening to your words in the context of the poem you are writing at the moment, you develop an instinct for suiting vocabulary to the poem. With regular practice you find that you home in on the words that fit most comfortably, and you can surprise yourself by choosing the best word without appearing to think about it.

Allow this instinct its head in the matter of word selection. You may find yourself writing words you really did not intend to put onto paper, and then realise that your instinct was guiding you into the right channel of thought. Such apparently random word choices may even spark off a new poem.

While thinking about sharing the washing-up with my sister, this phrase came into my mind and insisted on being written down:

> bonding ties
> one apron's string around us both

I was not planning to write a poem, just reflecting that each of us has her own home and family life, and the only time we ever work together is to tidy the kitchen after regular Sunday lunches at my parents' home.

The words, unconsidered and unbidden, prompted a poem and dictated the form it would take. 'Bonding' implies close links, and particularly the link between a mother and her child. 'Ties' reinforces the image. 'Apron's string' describes the physical item and echoes the cliché 'tied to a mother's apron strings.'

By sheer chance of unconscious word choice, a poem about ritual tasks and relationships almost wrote itself.

There are times when the best word simply will not present itself to you. When this happens, put down a substitute with similar meaning, and mark the substitute on your text. Do not strain after the right word. Go about your ordinary business letting your subconscious work on the problem for you. The chances are that the next time you turn to the poem the word you need will leap into your mind. If it does not, then wait a little longer. It is always worth taking time to find the one you want. If you allow the poem to be published with second best instead of the perfect word, it will glare at you every time you look at it.

Problem words

Use adverbs with caution. Although they may enhance your meaning, you can write with more precision by ignoring the adverb and seeking out a more effective verb.

Take, for example, the verb 'to eat'. It can be qualified by adverbs to draw different images. You could show somebody eating greedily, fussily, noisily or quickly. By thinking a little more about each action, you could show somebody gobbling, nibbling, munching or bolting his food. At once the image is clearer, and the picture in the reader's mind is more definite.

Adjectives need to be applied with similar care. An accurate adjective can colour a noun and bring the whole poem to life. Use too many, and your work becomes over rich and stodgy. The reader soon tires of a poem where every noun has to be qualified, and will focus his attention on the number of adjectives rather than on the piece itself.

There is a simple test which you can apply to your poem to check for this problem. First you score out every adjective in the piece. Ask yourself whether the poem is stronger or weaker as a result. Now allow yourself a single adjective. You might reinstate one you had lost, or find a new one. This exercise may confirm your original ideas, so that you feel the need to apply all the adjectives you had in the first place. If that is the case, do so. The exercise has proved that your first thoughts were correct. If, however, you find that the poem communicates well with fewer adjectives, you will see more clearly which should be removed and which remain.

Whatever the style of your poem, avoid archaic words. 'Whene'er', 'thou goest' and 'o'er' might have appealed to the Victorian reader, but you are writing today in the idiom of today. Current contractions such as 'don't' and 'aren't' are part of that idiom. 'Whene'er' is not. New words and changed usage of old words make up part of the vocabulary of modern poetry. If poetry were not allowed to move with its time, we should all be stuck in the style of Chaucer.

Pay particular attention to your use of the definite article. 'The' is a convenient word for poetry. There are numerous places where the poem would work whether or not it is included. It represents a useful device for keeping the rhythm of the piece tidy, occupying an unstressed syllable to maintain rhythmic balance. Because of the weight placed on every word, its repetitions glare at the reader and it assumes a far greater importance than it deserves.

Although 'the' has been singled out as a special case, you should remember that any word repeated within a poem draws attention to itself. Repetition is one of the devices that makes poetry memorable. If you repeat a word it will imprint itself firmly in the mind of the reader, so make sure that all repetitions are intentional, and not occasioned by sloppy thought.

An unconscious repetition may be remedied by consulting a thesaurus. where you will find a selection of words similar to the offending one. This form of word searching is anathema to some poets. They feel that any word which does not spring naturally from the mind to the page will make the poem seem forced. This need not be the case. In using a thesaurus, you are only bypassing a laborious process. And the word you find there will come under the same close scrutiny as every other when you reach the revision stage.

Be wary of using abstract words. They have a blurring effect on the poem, sapping its definition. Concrete words build up to form concrete images and so become more powerful and more memorable.

A poem speaking in general terms about love and loss and grief will not be as telling as one which portrays a real person grieving for another real person. A vague piece about joy will not communicate as strongly as one which explores genuine, joyful circumstances.

New ways with words

Language changes constantly. When it ceases to change, it becomes fossilised and dies, as in the case of Latin and ancient Greek. Poetry embraces the most innovative use of vocabulary, and the poet, the supreme lover of words, has the right and the responsibility to move the language forward.

In doing this, he taps into a special reserve of energy that fires his use of words and provides new excitements for himself and for his reader.

Be bold when you explore the language, and let your writing be full of experiments. Make a verb serve as a noun, mix your pronouns, qualify nouns with other nouns rather than adjectives.

These experiments will not all work. Some of them will make nonsense of your poem, but no matter. You are manipulating the language and testing its potential. You are laying down another store of experience.

Invent your own words, and use them in such a way that their context clarifies the meaning. This is not a new idea. Look at Lewis Carroll's poem 'Jabberwocky'. Much of its vocabulary would not be found in any dictionary, but the tenor of the poem tells the reader what the words mean. Use your new words frequently, and they could be assimilated into the language.

Seek out unusual similes. 'As cool as a cucumber' is expected, so try 'as cool as lunchtime's lasagne' or 'as cool as cracked vinyl'.

For greater effect, turn the similes into metaphors. Rather than describing A as being like B, make A become B. For example, the simile 'her smile was cold as cracked vinyl' could become the stronger metaphor 'cracked vinyl smile chilled her face'.

Once again be prepared for failed experiments, but remember that neglecting experimentation means a lack of innovation.

Word sounds

Remember that the words in your poem are going to be heard as well as read silently. Some poetry is destined to be spoken aloud to an audience; that which is read quietly by the individual still speaks out within his head. Use the sounds of the words you write to reinforce the message of your poem.

Be aware of onomatopoeia, allowing sound to indicate meaning. Try saying 'hiss', 'buzz', 'fly', 'cheer' and see how your voice imitates the action. Words which have this quality enhance the communication of the poem. Consider them when you are selecting your vocabulary.

Almost without noticing, the reader will infer a mood from your poem through your use of onomatopoeia. You can demonstrate the effect it has for yourself. Say 'bees buzzing, droning, humming', and tune in to the mood those sounds create. Say 'wood smoke rises, curling lazily', and listen to the different mood. Try 'nerves shivering, flesh creeping', and hear the contrast. By dropping these pearls of atmosphere into your writing, you are playing on the reader's imagination and fuelling his enjoyment of your work.

Note, too, the value of alliteration. Repeated consonant sounds also help to establish the mood of a poem, and that mood can vary to produce different effects depending on the other letters in the words. 'Languid liquid flow' and 'slithering, sliding, slipping' communicate very different images, even though the letter 'l' is repeated in each case.

Think about the length of sound in consonants. The sharper, plosive consonants (those whose pronunciation makes a miniature explosion of sound) produce a more percussive effect than sustained (or fricative) ones. So 'p', 't' and 'd' strike more crisply than 'f', 's' and 'm'. 'Tip top' is quicker and sharper to say than 'hiss soft', even though the same vowel sounds are used. Consider the effect on your poem of these categories of sound.

In order to illustrate that point, I used the same vowel sounds in each phrase, as vowels vary considerably in length. Take, for example, the letter 'a'. It produces different sounds in the words 'cat', 'calm', 'claim' and 'cairn'. But not only are the sounds themselves different, the syllable length also varies. So a line of poetry using short vowels and plosive consonants has an entirely different length from one with long vowels and sustained consonants, even when the same number of syllables occurs in each line.

Consider these two lines of ten syllables each in iambic pentameter.

1   He hit his head and broke a brittle bone.
2   She sleeps and dreams upon the flower-strewn ground.

Each example has ten syllables, but try saying them aloud and you will hear how much longer the second feels than the first. (Details of the metrical construction appear in the next chapter.)

It would be nonsense to suggest that these subtle aids to communication should appear in the first draft of a poem, or that you should hamper the flow of your ideas in order to analyse the words as you put them down. But when the surge of creativity is replaced by the more dispassionate analysis and revision process, do not undervalue the importance of the effect you create through sound.

Punctuation and grammar

If this heading makes you want to groan and skip the section, do not yield to temptation. The news is good. Although it helps to have an elementary knowledge of syntax, you do not need to be a grammatical genius to write poetry. If, however, you know nothing at all of the subject, it would be a good idea to learn from any basic text book. Mistakes made through ignorance will spoil the effect of your poem, whereas a deliberate departure from the rules can work for it.

The rules of grammar in prose apply to poetry, but your poem may be more telling if it flouts them. As long as your meaning is clear and communicates itself to the reader, eccentricities of grammar are acceptable.

Eccentricities for their own sake are an affectation. Where they work to enrich your poem, they are highly desirable. An unusual feature of style draws attention to itself and so heightens the reader's reaction.

There is one convention of grammar which may prove particularly helpful. Where a story breaks into a new paragraph, a poem opens a new stanza. This is a useful point to remember when you are writing free verse. Using a set form means that you have a pattern of line and stanza breaks. It can be difficult to tell where the new stanza begins when you do not have the framework of a set form. By pinpointing the shift that would indicate a new paragraph in prose, you are going to make sense of the breaks.

Capital letters in prose occur only after a full stop or at the beginning of a proper noun. In poetry you can use a capital letter at the start of each line if you wish, regardless of the punctuation at the end of the previous line. This is an option, not a rule. Free verse, more frequently follows the punctuation pattern of prose. Your instinct will tell you whether capitals or small letters are better in each of your poems.

e.e. cummings carried this option to the extreme by rejecting capital letters altogether. Neither the poetry nor the poet's status suffered.

Poetry allows you one form of punctuation which is unavailable in prose – the line break. In the distant past, poetry was end stopped, punctuated at the end of every line. Writers soon tired of such a restrictive style and nowadays a line or even a stanza may end with no punctuation, but run directly on into the next line. (This is known as an enjambement.)

This subtle pause, a mere suspension of breath when the poem is spoken, offers the perfect opportunity for you to impose a delicate emphasis on the final word of the line. Here is a stanza from a free verse poem about a child dying in a hospital ward. The enjambements of the first, second, fourth and fifth lines add the merest touch of weight and so draw the reader's attention to four rather ordinary words.

> We changed his linen
> before the other children woke, wondered
> if empty bed would hurt less than his pain.
> A check at dawn revealed
> indents in fresh sheets
> where earlier his trunk and limbs had pressed,
> head hollow on the pillow.

Sometimes a total absence of punctuation works. This is a particularly useful device when you wish to convey a sense of continuation or a feeling of harmony.

In the late 1960s the Liverpool poets took a lack of punctuation one step further by dropping some of the gaps between words, and binding two or more words together in an exciting combination.

When you reach the stage of revising your poem, look carefully at its punctuation. The spaces indicated can be as telling as the words that surround them. As with the words themselves, allow yourself to experiment with grammar and punctuation. Explore all the options to discover your own voice, and your poetry will come to life and speak out to communicate with everyone who reads it.

Exercises

3 For a week make a list of precise but unexpected phrases to describe things you see each day, and to describe the emotions you feel or observe in others. (Remember to store your best descriptions in your notebook.)

4 Read any contemporary poem and mark every adjective, adverb and definite article it uses. Look back at them and ask yourself whether you would have used those constructions or whether you can think of better substitutes.

5 Invent a new word to convey each of the following: fear, joy, anger, boredom, speed, gluttony.

6 Return to the notes, words and phrases from Exercises 1 and 2. Can you find any stronger or more appropriate ways of expressing yourself?

4

RHYTHM AND METRE

Rhythm surrounds every part of our lives. Before we are born we are comforted by the regular throb of our mother's heartbeat, and as babies we are reassured by being rocked back and forth. There is rhythm in the pulsing of blood around the body, the changing motions of the earth producing day and night cycles, and the passage of the seasons. There is rhythm in the regularity of the tide, the waxing and waning of the moon, in the wave patterns through which light and sound travel.

It is not surprising that poetry, which is close to the roots of existence, should be full of rhythm, the flow of stressed and unstressed syllables through language.

Perhaps more than rhyme, rhythm makes poetry memorable for its speaker and holds the attention of the listener, which were vital considerations in the days of the oral tradition. But as well as being useful as a means of prompting memory and gripping an audience, a pleasing rhythm quite simply makes words more attractive to listen to.

Small children learn to apply the skills of language through rhythm. As soon as youngsters can pronounce recognisable words and phrases, they start to learn nursery rhymes, many of which are accompanied by regular movements (e.g. Pat-a-cake baker's man, See-saw Margery Daw). The strong rhythms instil an element of fun. And, while the children play, they are practising memory techniques, handling vocabulary, absorbing cadences of their language with its alternating stressed and unstressed syllables, and discovering grammatical constructions.

Apart from its pleasurable aspect, there is also an innate power in rhythm, which throbs through our mind and reverberates in our imagination. Traditionally, chants and incantations have been used to invoke magical or supernatural responses. A strongly rhythmical piece, however short, puts its message across. Countless consumer products are advertised with rhythmic slogans.

Rhythm maintains the intensity of a poem, carrying it from writer to reader. The writer's intentions are less likely to be misunderstood if appropriate rhythms flow through the poem. Rhythm also reinforces the subject matter and applies a particular tone to the piece.

Rhythm is the most profound way to achieve effects in sound. The sound of a poem, its beats and cadences, has a strong emotional effect on the writer who creates the poem and the reader who enjoys it. This is part of the music of poetry, which has the power to move and excite as well as narrate a story and create an atmosphere.

As well as contributing to its music, rhythm is part of the completeness of the poem. Its insistence tells the reader that there is more to come, and its ultimate and satisfying conclusion rounds the poem strongly and beautifully.

Metre

If the word 'metre' conjures up for you memories of scanning chunks of Virgil for Latin exams and ruining your earliest experiences of Shakespeare, you may prefer to omit this section. I believe it is possible to write powerful and meaningful free verse poetry without knowing anything at all about metre; but a study of metre in contemporary poetry can enhance your enjoyment of reading and make easier the business of writing poems. If you wish to write poetry in set forms, it is essential.

Metre is the pattern of poetic composition dictated by the type and number of measures (FEET) in a line. The order of accented and unaccented syllables gives the style of each foot. In the examples given in this section, / denotes an accented syllable and X denotes an unaccented syllable.

Iambic metre

The way we pronounce the English language makes an iambic metre the easiest to use when we write. This is where every second syllable is stressed. One iambic foot, or iambus, consists of an unstressed syllable followed by a stressed one. Each of these words is one iambus:

X / X / X / X /
before again demand ascend

Of course, poems are not created solely out of words of two syllables with that particular stress pattern. Let us consider an iambic line, using five feet, and so referred to as iambic pentameter.

X / X / X / X / X /
Before you left I spoke your name again

Two of the words in this line have already been described as iambic, and 'before' and 'again' each represent one foot. The other three feet are each made up of two single-syllable words. Now consider this example:

X / X / X / X / X /
If only I was standing here with you

Once more most of the words are monosyllabic, and just two words consist of two syllables; but here the words of two syllables are split for scansion purposes. The first syllable of each word joins the one before it to form an iambus, while each second syllable links with the one after it to form the next iambus.

When longer words are used, the natural stresses of the language share out their syllables among the five feet. Eg:

X / X / X / X / X /
Whenever anybody interjects

Here each word contains one complete iambus. 'Whenever' and 'interjects' have one extra syllable each which links with the extra syllables in 'anybody'. The iambus within 'anybody' falls in the second and third syllables of the word, while the first and fourth link with those extra syllables from the other two words. A standard line of iambic pentameter has ten syllables which fall naturally into alternating unstressed and stressed syllables. For the purposes of metre, the length of each individual word is unimportant as long as the beat is correct and the total syllabic count comes to ten. Lines of unrhymed iambic pentameter are known as blank verse.

Introducing variety

If you write a sequence of lines in iambic pentameter as described, you will see that an over-strict adherence to the metre makes for very dull reading. The reassurance of a steady beat soon becomes an irritation, and the regular thump of the stressed syllable reverberates in a listener's ear long after the meaning of the words has slipped away.

Although I use the word 'listener', this effect is not restricted to people hearing a poem spoken aloud. For as we read silently to ourselves, we still 'hear' the words spoken in our head. An uncompromisingly regular beat hammers as strongly from the page as it does through the medium of someone else's voice.

In order to bring some variety into the lines, you can make slight deviations from the expected pattern of stresses. You can incorporate an extra syllable or omit one. You can substitute a different style of foot for the usual iambus.

Apart from variations in the stress pattern, you can adjust the effect of the beat by using pauses, allowing punctuation to alter the flow of the lines. You can use lines of a different length from an expected pentameter on a regular or occasional basis. Let us consider some lines in iambic pentameter by William Shakespeare, whose plays are probably the most widely known writings in this form. Juliet uses standard, unvaried iambic pentameter when she says to Romeo:

If thou dost love, pronounce it faithfully:
Or if thou think'st I am too quickly won,

I'll frown and be perverse and say thee nay.

There is a fluent, poetical feel to these lines; but in the next, a tiny change in balance adds pleasing variety:

× / × / × / / × × /
So thou wilt woo; but else, not for the world.

The sense and natural cadence of this line indicates that 'not for' does not follow the expected pattern of an unstressed syllable followed by a stressed one. It would read more appropriately if the 'not' were stressed and the 'for' unstressed. In other words, Shakespeare has brought variety into the passage by changing one iambus into its mirror image, a *trochee*.

We see the same variation in Hamlet's famous speech which begins:

> To be, or not to be, that is the question:
> Whether 'tis nobler in the mind to suffer
> The slings and arrows of outrageous fortune,
> Or to take arms against a sea of troubles,
> And by opposing end them? . . .

The second and fourth lines open with this trochaic substitution. The pronunciation of 'whether' indicates a pattern of stressed followed by unstressed syllable, and the sense of 'or to' gives the same indication.

In addition to this, there is an extra unstressed syllable (feminine ending) at the end of each line. This provides more variety in the pattern of the iambic pentameter, but its presence does something else. It reinforces the mood of hesitation and questioning that pervades the speech.

So while it is highly desirable to ring the changes in metrical pattern, this is not a haphazard process. Experiment by writing lines in iambic pentameter, and experiment further by exploring for yourself the effects that variations in the pattern can produce.

There is a perceptible difference between variations incorporated in the metre of a poem to enhance its message and those imposed merely for the sake of introducing variety. In the same way, there is a vast difference between metrical lines that use deviations from metre for considered effect and those produced by a writer whose grasp of metre is inadequate.

Other metres

Of course, iambic pentameter is by no means the only medium for producing metrical poetry. Lines may be of different lengths, and feet may be of different stress patterns. Unless you are writing in a set form that demands a particular metre, allow the subject matter of your poem and the words themselves to set their pattern. Consider these line lengths:

monometer	1 foot per line
dimeter	2 feet
trimeter	3 feet
tetrameter	4 feet
pentameter	5 feet
hexameter	6 feet
heptameter	7 feet
octameter	8 feet

Monometer is seldom used throughout a long poem for the obvious reason that it becomes tedious to read, although a short piece with just one foot on a line may carry a telling message. It is more frequently found in occasional use, perhaps as the chorus line of a poem which relies on a longer standard line.

Dimeter and trimeter are seen more often although they are still fairly short lines.

Tetrameter, like pentameter, allows latitude for development and variation within the line.

Hexameter is the length used in Latin and Greek epic verse. You may see a line of iambic hexameter referred to as an alexandrine. Like heptameter (sometimes called the ballad line because it is frequently used in that format), hexameter has an extended feel about it which gives an almost conversational, narrative mood to a line.

33

Octameter is the longest form to be endowed with a length name, and is not seen very often. It is more usual for a line of this length to be written in the form of two shorter ones, but there are occasions when the atmosphere of the poem demands the unbroken effect of such a long line.

Different feet

All of these lengths individually, and combinations of them, allow you to write metrical poetry with line lengths to suit different moods. Their effectiveness can be enhanced by careful choice of the style of foot. Consider these feet:

2-syllable feet

iambus	✕ /	report, amaze
trochee	/ ✕	careful, whether
pyrrhic	✕ ✕	in a, to the
spondee	/ /	full flow, pack horse

3-syllable feet

anapaest	✕ ✕ /	recommend, up a tree
dactyl	/ ✕ ✕	character, paperback
amphibrach	✕ / ✕	forgetful, depending
amphimacer	/ ✕ /	cap in hand, yesterday
bacchic	/ / ✕	blue heaven, sea bathing
anti-bacchic	✕ / /	an old dress, by deep streams
tribrach	✕ ✕ ✕	if it is, and as a
molossus	/ / /	ball point pen, wild grey sea.

Some lists go on to detail the subtleties of 4-syllable feet. For the poet's practical purposes, a knowledge of 2- and 3-syllable feet is sufficient.

Metrical poetry uses either one style of foot or a combination of two or more in regular patterns to strengthen its effectiveness. As we have already seen, the English language flows easily in iambic feet, and the slight shift of balance to the trochaic foot is equally fluent. These examples show the difference between iambic and trochaic tetrameter:

```
X / X  /  X  /  X /
I go to watch the ships today,
X   /   X   /  X / X  /
To watch them ride the angry sea. (iambic)
```

```
 / X  /  X / X  /  X
Going down today and watching
 /  X  /  X  / X  / X
Ships that ride the angry waters. (trochaic)
```

Although the meaning is the same, the stress pattern of each example imprints a different beat through its use of metre, and so imposes a subtle difference of mood. The effect of a metrical pattern incorporating a three-syllable foot is more tripping:

```
 / X  X  / X  / X  X  /  X
Faster than fairies, faster than witches,
 /  X X  / X  / X  X  /  X
Bridges and houses, hedges and ditches
```

Robert Louis Stevenson's poem 'From a Railway Carriage' reflects the motion of a train through the beat of the dactyls and trochees.

In Byron's 'Destruction of Sennacherib' we see the galloping rhythm of the anapaest:

```
X  X / X  X   /  X  X  /  X  X  /
The Assyrian came down like the wolf on the fold,
```

```
X  X  /  X   X   /   X X  / X X   /
```
And his cohorts were gleaming in purple and gold;

The chanting effect of the amphibrach is demonstrated in the anonymous line:
```
X   /  X  X  /  X  X   /   X   X  /  X
```
Remember, remember the fifth of November

Tennyson used a heavier metre in 'The Charge of the Light Brigade':

```
/  X  /     /  X  /
```
Half a league, half a league,
```
/  X  /    /   X
```
Half a league onward

The amphimacers and trochee hold the rhythm of the horses, but carry an ominous weight appropriate to the poem's message.

It is useful to experiment with metre and discover all its effects through your own poetry as well as in the writing of others. Only when you have explored and played with the different line lengths and styles of feet can their relevance to poetry be fully understood.

A study of metre should be approached not as a hurdle that has to be overcome, but as a device for strengthening the meaning of a poem. Nor should metre be an item on a checklist for the appreciation of poetry. When carefully used, metre should slip by unnoticed at a first reading; only a deeper analysis reveals the way in which it becomes part of the magic of a good poem.

Shelley's poetry speaks its powerful message, and yet his notebooks reveal that the beat of each poem often arrived before the words. Marking out the metre is a good way of checking that the poem fits into the pattern determined for it, a way of reining in the ideas to prevent them from running out of control and so losing direction.

Gerard Manley Hopkins perhaps came closest to bridging the gap between strictly metred poetry and free verse with his sprung rhythm. This concentrates on the measuring of stressed syllables. These may stand alone (as a monosyllabic foot) or be accompanied by one, two or three unstressed syllables to form the foot. Feet may span from one line into the next. His poetry has a profound sense of rhythm without chiming regularity.

For some writers, the discipline of metre is an essential part of the task of composition. For some it is anathema. Others will allow the poem they are writing to dictate whether or not metre should be applied.

Whichever path you choose to tread, do not deny the relevance of the others, or the usefulness of experimenting with different feet and lengths. Consider the value of an appreciation of metre. It may be far from your mind during the flow of creativity, and yet a check on it when you have finished helps your assessment of the piece you have produced. Above all remember that metre does not have to be your master, but an understanding of how it works can add an extra dimension to your writing.

Exercises

7 Allow yourself just three minutes to think of and write down all the advertising slogans you can remember. Look back at them to see how many rely on strong rhythm to convey a message, and note which other devices of poetry are used, such as rhyme or repetition. Consider the powerful effects of poetry inferred from your list.

8. Use the rhythm of music to promote a flow of words by making up an extra verse for a song or hymn. You do not have to follow the sense of the rest of the song – merely fit into its rhythm.

9 Write a sequence of unrhymed lines in iambic pentameter on the subject of your present or childhood home. Include physical details and your own emotions.

10 Go back to the notes on an ancient building from Exercise 2 (modified in Exercise 6). Use the notes as source material for a number of lines written in different lengths and using different feet. Does any pattern prompt you to develop it into a poem?

5

RHYME

Like rhythm, rhyme helps to make a poem memorable and adds to the beauty of its sound, but a poem can work as a vibrant and artistic piece of writing without any rhyme at all.

As poets writing today, we are fortunate in having a wide range of options in rhyme available to us. No longer need we feel hemmed in by the constrictions of strict patterns of rhyme. There are more subtle rhyming effects we can use.

Poets will, of course, have preferences for rhymed or unrhymed work, but this does not mean that you should be categorised neatly as a rhyming or non-rhyming writer. An awareness of the range of styles available helps you to select the best one for each poem.

Rhyme has a cumulative effect on a poem. A single pair of rhyming words does not chime very strongly, but a repeated pattern of rhyme resounds in the reader's mind and reinforces the structure of the poem.

This is particularly true of slant rhymes, those which do not fall into the full rhyme category but where similarity of sound produces a special unity.

There is slant rhyming in 'stoop' and 'steep', or in 'mole' and 'code', or 'riding' and 'beside'. One or two slant rhymes of this type could pass unnoticed, as a chance similarity in sound produced by the pronunciation of the language. Repeated use of slant rhymes gives the poem a sense of cohesion and dynamism.

Strict rhyme, like strict rhythm, makes a piece of writing instantly identifiable as poetry rather than prose. Subtle poetry repeats itself in terms of both rhyme and rhythm until its message penetrates. Once it has made itself heard, the message is not likely to be forgotten.

Watch out for unintentional rhyming within your poem. Your vocabulary may offer a word that would be absolutely correct in its context; but if it happens to rhyme, either fully or slantwise, with the sounds around it, it will draw far too much attention to itself and break the pattern of rhyme you are creating. Under these circumstances it is better to sacrifice the unintentionally rhyming word and substitute another.

The particular effect you create by means of rhyme may not be the same when the poem is read silently as when it is spoken aloud. While you are writing it is important to read over your work both silently and out loud in order to appreciate the direction the poem is taking. As well as allowing you to listen to the effects of your use of rhyme, this shows up flaws which need to be corrected and areas where the overall balance of the poem is not pleasing.

Whether you are using full or slant rhymes it is important to remember that the sense of what you are saying is paramount. Never stretch the meaning of your writing merely to make use of a good rhyme. If you cannot find an appropriate rhyme for a particular word, change that word to one which does have a suitable rhyme.

Full rhyme

In full rhyme, the final sounds of the words are the same. 'Moon' and 'June' are full rhymes, as are 'me' and 'see', and 'pot' and 'spot'.

Full rhyme firmly establishes a piece of work as a poem in the mind of the reader. But, because the number of rhyming words is finite and limited, it is easy to fall into the trap of writing rhyme clichés. 'Moon' and 'June' have already been quoted, but it is tempting to let people in love look at the stars above and gulls fly free over the sparkling sea. If you want your poem to sound original, be sure to put such temptation behind you.

If you are writing poetry in a set form that requires a number of rhymes to be found for each sound, be careful to chose vocabulary that will allow you the greatest possible list of alternatives. For example, an Italian sonnet requires two sets of four rhyming words in the first eight lines. If you choose to end your first two lines with 'orange' and 'business', you will have a lot of trouble simply finding three more rhymes for each, regardless of whether or not such rhyming words make sense.

If you enjoy writing rhymed poetry, invest in a rhyming dictionary. These have been condemned by some writers, who feel that their use is totally artificial, that a word which does not spring naturally to mind will never fit into the poem. By using one carefully you can bypass the tedious task of sifting through options, and discover alternatives which might never have occurred to you otherwise. You can also see at a glance lists of words with different numbers of syllables. Before starting to write you can check how many words rhyme with a particular sound, and whether they are likely to be of use in your poem.

Unless you are writing in set forms that require rhymes to appear at a fixed point, normally at the end of a line, experiment with rhymes in unexpected places. Discover the effect of using two or three words with full rhyme in the same line. Try rhyming the first words of your lines instead of the last. Vary the frequency of your rhymes to make an interesting pattern. For example, you might have lines 1 and 2 rhyming together, 3 and 8 rhyming, 4 and 6 rhyming, 5 and 10 rhyming, etc. When you start writing a poem in this way it feels chaotic and false, but the unifying effect of rhyme soon begins to work, and the sound is pleasing and more subtle than regular, full rhyme.

One style, however, which cries out for regular, full rhyme is humorous writing. Frequent rhyme coupled with strong rhythm gives the bounce that tells the reader the poem is funny well before he reaches the punchline. It is possible to write humorous poetry without rhyme, of course, but you have to work a lot harder to achieve your effect.

An extreme example of full rhyme is complete repetition, where the full word recurs instead of just the final sound. Unless a poem's set form demands this repetition it may sound unsatisfying, even when the word is spelt differently and has a different meaning. For example:

> I gripped my little horse's rein
> And cantered on through wind and rain . . .

is not a comfortable rhyme to accept, even though it makes sense.

> I gripped my little horse's rein
> And cantered on along the lane . . .

also makes sense, and is a more readily acceptable rhyme.

In some cases complete repetition helps build the atmosphere of a poem. Its particularly strong sound-echo produces an almost hypnotic effect, but it should be used with caution.

Slant rhyme

There is a pleasing resonance about slant rhyme, an echo of sound which is insistent but never strident. It arises from similarity of sound that is close enough to produce a suggestion of rhyme without chiming. It hints gently instead of hammering its message home.

Assonance is a form of rhyme where identical, stressed vowel sounds appear with different consonants. Where full rhyme would pair 'sleep' with 'deep', assonance pairs 'sleep' with 'dream' or 'wheat' or 'feed'. For example:

> No night passed when we did not feed
> Our hungry minds on broken dreams . . .

Its opposite, consonance, occurs when the consonant sounds following stressed vowel sounds remain the same, such as the pairing of 'feel' with 'call'. For example:

> . . . where nobody could feel
> his loss or hear his call . . . .

Full consonance is when the consonant sounds at each end of a stressed vowel sound are identical, pairing 'feel' with 'fall', or 'wash' with 'wish'.

Alliteration – the repetition of consonant sounds in close or adjacent words – instils an aura of rhyme. For example:

> Sweet sleep stifles thought, forces phantoms to fly.

Of course, the consonants may be produced by different letters. The same sound occurs at the beginning of 'forces' and of 'phantoms'.

Crossed syllable rhyming is found where one syllable of one word rhymes with a different syllable of another, as in the 'ave' sound of 'behaviour' and 'gravely'. Although the effect of this device is slight, its repeated use helps to reinforce the poem. For example:

> . . . one word about behaviour
> could make us all act gravely . . .

Sight rhyme is more pleasing to the eye than the ear. It consists of words which do not have the same pronunciation, but are spelt in the same way, such as 'cough' and 'through' or 'sties' and 'penalties'.

Wrenched, or synthetic rhyme, as its name suggests, contorts the pronunciation of the language in order to produce a rhyme. For example:

> A few days later
> I went to the the-atre

This device works splendidly for comic effect but should be used with caution in more serious poems.

Unaccented rhyme ignores the stressed syllables of the words, but produces rhyme in unstressed syllables, as in 'manner' and 'better'.

Half rhyme occurs when the stressed syllables of words rhyme fully and the following unstressed syllables are different; for example, 'wilful' and 'killing', or 'indolence' and 'indicate'.

Another form of slant rhyme pairs a stressed with an unstressed syllable. For example:

> Down by the sea
> We were all making merry . . .

Feminine rhyme consists of a full rhyme followed by rhyming

unaccented syllables; for example, 'spelling' and 'telling', or 'planet' and 'Janet'.

You will see that there is no shortage of options available to the poet who wants to include an element of rhyme in his work while avoiding the weight of full rhyme.

Incidentally, while you are considering these dynamic sound patterns, do not forget the value of onomatopoeia in creating atmosphere. When you use words whose meaning is reinforced by the sound they make when spoken aloud, the mood of your poem gains a subtle underlining.

Syllabics

Although not a rhyme form, syllabic poetry is enjoyable to write and pleasing to hear. Its unity depends not on the repetition of similar or identical sounds, as in rhyme, but on the repeated pattern of a count of syllables, regardless of whether they are stressed or unstressed. It is the traditional Japanese and Celtic style of writing poetry, and appears in much of Dylan Thomas' work. Syllabic poetry falls into one of three categories.

Normative syllabics is a form where every line of the poem has the same number of syllables.

In quantitative syllabics the count varies from line to line within the first stanza. Following stanzas all repeat the pattern laid down in the first.

Variable syllabics allow line lengths to vary at random, but the poet sets limits and keeps within them. For example, no line in a poem may have fewer than four syllables or more than nine.

Unrhymed verse

One of the questions most frequently asked about unrhymed or free verse is how it may be distinguished from prose. There is no easy answer to this. You can say that poetry, whether free or rhymed, is written in lines and stanzas rather than paragraphs, but this makes no allowance for the message of the piece, or vocabulary selection. A wordy poem may sound less like poetry than a tightly written piece of prose.

A poem presents an idea, a story, a picture, perhaps, in its entirety. A prose passage can do the same.

Poetry communicates a message, via the medium of language, from its writer to its reader. Prose can do the same.

Poetry reaches deeply to touch its writer and its reader at a profound level of emotion. Prose can do the same.

In other words, the acceptance of a piece of free verse as poetry rather than prose is subjective. You must choose for yourself whether you are looking at poetry or prose. Instinct tells you that you are dealing with poetry, but that instinct can be honed by wide and regular reading of poetry so that it recognises the form at first glance.

Free verse should never be regarded as the easy option by a writer who has no interest in the rhyming or rhythmic structures of poetry. In fact, it is more difficult to write a good free verse poem than you may think, because you need to establish your writing as poetry without the supporting presence of rhyme.

If you choose to adopt a regular metrical pattern, your piece will have the feel of poetry about it. If you reject metre as well as rhyme, your task is doubly difficult.

By letting the piece you are writing dictate to you whether it should be a rhymed or free-verse poem, you are unlikely to make a mistake in this basic area of choice. Keep your mind open and keep your options open. Let the poem surprise you by its preference for full, slant or absence of rhymes.

Exercises

11 Without worrying about producing complete poems, write a series of phrases and lines that use the different techniques of slant rhyme. Does any particular effect please you? If so, expand on it by producing more lines using the same effect. (These may build up into a complete poem.)

12 Using the theme of imprisonment write a short, strictly rhymed

poem and then a piece of free verse. Which pleases you more? Which allies its theme more closely to its style of rhyme? Did you expect your answer to the last question, or was it a surprise?

13 Spend half an hour looking through any book or magazine of contemporary poetry. Analyse the rhyming patterns or absence of them in a selection of pieces. Do you think that rhyme devices are used successfully or not?

14 Take any poem you have written in the past and check the rhyme style you have used, whether full, slant or free. If you had used rhyme before, try writing the same poem in free verse. If the original is in free verse, try writing the same poem with rhyme.

15 Go back to the lines you produced in Exercise 9. Alter these to accommodate a pattern of slant rhyme at the ends of the lines. Your rhymes may occur in a regular or random pattern.

6

FORM

There is no such thing as formless poetry. As soon as words start appearing on paper, they take on a pattern. Writing poetry involves putting down words in more or less ordered patterns to produce interesting effects. Over the centuries many of these patterns have caught the imagination of writers and become set, to be used and re-used to communicate to readers.

This has led to the creation of a huge reservoir of set forms and widely used variations on them. (Lewis Turco's *The New Book of Forms* lists more than two hundred and fifty.) The list is still growing, and will continue to grow as long as people are writing poetry. For poets want to put a unique stamp on their work and to adapt set forms to suit their own purposes.

For this reason, although traditional forms remain fixed in their original blueprint, new adaptations of them appear constantly. Only history will tell which of these variations catch the imagination of poets and become set forms for succeeding generations who will, of course, add variations of their own. So a form that is set is by no means static.

You may wish to write a poem in a particular form for practice, or because the form holds some appeal for you, or perhaps the theme or first few lines you produce will lead you into a suitable pattern. Having chosen a form, you will need to decide just how closely you want to adhere to it.

It is not only permissible but positively recommended to use some latitude in form. A strictly produced poem without the tiniest movement away from the expected stress or rhyme pattern would be dull. Counterpoint adds variety and interest, but be warned. There is a big difference between counterpoint used for good effect and deviation from set patterns appearing because the poet was insufficiently competent to handle his form. If you ever find yourself thinking that this or that word does not quite fit, and yet decide to leave it in because you cannot come up with a better one, your poem will shout at its reader that it has not been handled correctly. A deliberate use of slant rhyme where full was expected, or unstressed beat where the reader thought he would find a stressed one, communicates a subtle message and insinuates pleasing variety.

However subtly you use variations, too many of them will sap the strength of your chosen form, so use them sparingly.

Experiment with old forms, imposing new rules of your own on to them, and also try constructing new forms. Consider the balance of line and stanza, of rhyme and metre. Note the distinctive style of each form, and think about the subject matter which would lend itself to treatment in that style.

Look at the experimental work produced by other poets. For example, American writer Dr Alfred Dorn has devised a series of polymetrical verse forms, using a combination of different metres in a more or less rigid fashion.

This experimentation has a ludic quality, an element of 'fun and games' which should be encouraged. We all need to play games with our writing, through which we broaden our experience of poetry. And there is always the chance that one of our games will become a standardised form.

Consider some of the best-known forms, given here with examples. Unfortunately it is necessary to resort to 'poetspeak' in order to explain the forms, but the examples should help make sense of the jargon.

The terms used to define metre are those detailed in Chapter 4, and rhyme schemes are given alphabetically. This means that the first word to rhyme with anything is referred to as 'a', and all further rhymes with the same sound are called 'a'. The next rhyming sound to be introduced is 'b', along with all of its rhymes, the third sound is 'c', and so on. When a full or part line is repeated rather than merely ending with a rhyme, the upper case is used, ie. 'A', 'B'. If two lines that rhyme together are repeated, they become 'A1' and 'A2'. Words which do not have associated rhymes are given the letter 'x' in the following examples. (All this is easier to see in practice than to appreciate from an explanation.)

Some well known forms

Couplets

A couplet is simply a pairing of two lines. You can compose a poem of these used consecutively or broken into two-line stanzas, with any line length, any metre, and full, slant or no rhyme.

Metrical, rhyming couplets are frequently used in humorous verse:

'Twas the night before Christmas, the season of peace,	a
When all should be merry save turkeys and geese.	a
But despite their intentions to rest, share goodwill,	b
One family found there was work to do still.	b
Mum had bought all the presents a month back or more,	c
But still they were scattered, unwrapped, on the floor.	c
The kids cut the paper in pieces too small . . . etc	d

The rhymed couplet is rather a restricted form because of the proximity of the rhyming words, but fun to try.

Quatrains

A quatrain is a group of four lines, possibly a complete poem in itself or a stanza from a longer poem. As with couplets, you may use any pattern of line length, rhyme and metre, but some patterns of quatrain have become established as set forms.

Ballad Stanza

This is a quatrain, usually in iambic metre, with four feet in the first and third lines, and three feet in the second and fourth lines. The second and fourth lines rhyme. The shorter lines may be indented.

No matter that the bell had rung	x
To summon her to school,	a
She caught a bus the other way,	x
And broke the teacher's rule.	a

FORM

Kyrielle

The kyrielle is a French form dating from the Middle Ages, and is often used in hymns. It may be written in couplet or quatrain stanzas, but because it carries a refrain in the last line of each stanza, it is a most difficult poem to write convincingly in couplets. The refrain may be a whole line, a single word or a phrase.

In couplet form its rhyme scheme is a A, a A, a A etc., while the four-line form may rhyme either a a b B, c c b B, d d b B, etc., or a b a B, c b c B, d b d B etc. Iambic tetrameter is usually used.

Dim shadows, moving through the past	a
jolt me, and memories flooding fast	a
swamp all my thoughts. I fix my eye	b
beyond the clouds to dark, full sky.	B
No man shall ever touch my dreams;	c
my veins bleed dust of arid streams.	c
No man shall ever hear my cry	b
beyond the clouds to dark, full sky . . .	B

OR

This is the perfect winter day	a
with wind to wisp the clouds, a glare	b
of low sun breaking from the grey,	a
a hint of frost to charge the air	B
No time to linger; hurry down	c
familiar paths through woods to where	b
green icy waves, unceasing, pound	c
and fling their spume to charge the air . . .	B

Rubai

This quatrain form is Arabic, and has a delicate rhyme pattern of a a x a, b b x b, c c x c etc. It is written in iambic tetrameter or pentameter.

The Moving Finger Writes; and, having writ,	a

49

Moves on: nor all your Piety nor Wit	a
Shall lure it back to cancel half a Line,	x
Nor all your Tears wash out a Word of it	a

(from Edward Fitzgerald's translation of The Rubaiyat of Omar Khayyam.)

Interlocking rubais (or rubaiyat) make the third line of each stanza rhyme with the first, second and fourth lines of the next, a a b a, b b c b, c c d c etc. The third line of the last stanza picks up the sound of the first line of the poem. Robert Frost's 'Stopping by Woods on a Snowy Evening' is an excellent example of this form.

Pantoum

The pantoum is a Malayan verse form which was first used in Europe at the beginning of the nineteenth century.

It is written as a series of quatrains with lines of any single length and metre. There may be any number of stanzas, but lines two and four of each are repetons; that is, appear once more in their entirety. They become lines one and three of the next stanza. The second and fourth lines of the final stanza are, respectively, the third and first lines of the first stanza, producing a pattern of A1 B1 A2 B2, B1 C1 B2 C2, C1 D1 C2 D2 etc, until the final stanza Z1 A2 Z2 A1. Sometimes the final stanza is a couplet instead of the regular quatrain, and has the pattern A2 A1.

Still Journeying

It came to pass an age ago,	A1
the journey of those nightmare days.	B1
Now there is nothing left to show,	A2
no star where we can fix our gaze.	B2
The journey of those nightmare days	B1
held promises of coming light.	C1
No star where we can fix our gaze	B2
remains to prove the sky-child's might.	C2
Held promises of coming light	C1

filtered away as grains of sand,	D1
remains to prove the sky-child's might	C2
all blown as dust across the land.	D2
Filtered away as grains of sand,	D1
the gifts we gave are lost. Our prayer	E1
all blown as dust across the land,	D2
ignored; we ask from deep despair.	E2
The gifts we gave are lost, our prayer	E1
forgotten. Is our ancient pride	F1
ignored? We ask from deep despair	E2
if birth was born, or if death died.	F2
Forgotten is our ancient pride.	F1
Now there is nothing left to show	A2
if birth was born or if death died.	F2
It came to pass an age ago.	A1

The pantoum is a form for those who enjoy crosswords and jigsaws. Its tight pattern of repetitions makes it restricting, but the claustrophobic effect gives a haunting, obsessional feel to the poem.

Triolet
A brief form, just eight lines long, the triolet originated in France. The first line recurs at lines four and seven, and the second reappears as the last line. There are only two rhymes: A B a A a b A B. Iambic pentameter or tetrameter is generally used.

Whirlpool

Wild water whirls in circles, swirls	A
and drags its surface down to caverns; deep	B
beneath the crystal bubble columns, pearls	a
wild water. Whirls in circles, swirls,	A
froths, eddies thrust out crested plumes and curls	a
to draw each living thing to lasting sleep.	b
Wild water whirls in circles, swirls	A
and drags its surface down to caverns deep.	B

Although the slightness of this form lends itself to a cameo of description or a humourous verse, it can be used as a vehicle for more weighty ideas.

Chaucerian Roundel

Two lines longer than the triolet, this form allows a little more development of ideas but keeps just two rhymes and full line repetition. It was developed by Chaucer from the French roundel (described below).

It consists of three stanzas, the first line recurring at the end of the second and third stanzas. Its rhyme scheme is A b b, a b A, a b b A. The two examples show a Chaucerian roundel written in iambic tetrameter, (the most common metre along with iambic pentameter) and, for fun, the same rhyme scheme constructed in free metre. This indicates how the mood of the form can be changed by varying the metrical pattern.

Manhunt

You have to kiss a lot of frogs	A
before you find a handsome prince	b
Mere froggy speech will not convince	b
this princess to search under logs	a
and lily pads. It makes me wince,	b
to have to kiss a lot of frogs.	A
It could be worse, if rats or hogs	a
were forms used to disguise a prince.	b
But I shall not be looking, since	b
you have to kiss a lot of frogs.	A

OR

Birdwatching

Lurking in the fold where the curtain falls	A
she uses her cover to spy	b
on birds that swoop and wheel across the sky.	b

Ears twitch, eyes follow; she ignores our calls   a
to food and milk and company,   b
lurking in the fold where the curtain falls.   A

She stretches, arches, turns and sprawls   a
in parody of nonchalance; her eye   b
and ear intent still on each glide and cry –   b
lurking in the fold where the curtain falls.   A

Rondel
This is a medieval French form, and although early rondels are found in English poetry, they became popular in the nineteenth century.

Once again we find only two rhyming sounds in the form, and again the first and second lines are refrains (recurring at precise intervals more than once in the poem.) The standard rondel has fourteen lines of any single length and metre divided into three stanzas, and rhymes either A B b a, a b A B, a b b a A B or A B a b, b a A B, a b a b A B.

14th April, 1912

The people thought their rescuers would come.   A
This ship was safer than the frozen sea,   B
so passengers ignored the Captain's plea.   b
Unsinkable, this ship would not succumb.   a

Ripped open by the ice, she still had some   a
faint hope of floating. They would soon be free,   b
the people thought. Their rescuers would come,   A
This ship was safer than the frozen sea.   B

Iced inrush jarred her equilibrium   a
until she foundered. Then too late to flee   b
her passengers screamed their last agony,   b
fell silent as a black flood struck them dumb.   a
The people thought their rescuers would come –   A
this ship was safer than the frozen sea.   B

Rondels may have just thirteen lines, taking the same form as the full version but repeating either A or B at the end instead of both lines. (Some books, particularly American texts, refer to the thirteen-line form as the rondel and the fourteen-liner as the rondel supreme.)

Rondeau

Another form originating in France, the rondeau also has three stanzas, but features a refrain which picks up the first word or phrase of the poem. The full lines, none of which is repeated, may be of any single length and metre. The rhyme scheme is a a b b a, a a b R, a a b b a R (where R represents 'refrain').

Silver Ring Rondeau

I dropped my ring; watched ripples crease a line	a
of iced black water, give the only sign	a
of movement in the stillness of this cave.	b
I stooped, as if I thought that I could save	b
my ring from slipping through earth's fissured spine	a
In truth, my clumsiness was by design.	a
The subterranean channels of the mine	a
were tomb black, hushed and colder than the grave.	b
I dropped my ring.	R
When I am long gone, then my ring will shine,	a
reborn and new discovered, crystalline	a
reminder I once trod this timeless wave	b
whose tide change grips us all. For this I gave	b
your gift, full circle, love and soul entwined.	a
I dropped my ring	R

Terza Rima

As its name suggests, this is an Italian verse form, and was used by Dante in his Divine Comedy. It is chain rhymed (i.e. carrying a rhyming sound from one stanza to the next), an effect which gives a delightful flow and is comparatively easy to use. It is written in tercets (stanzas of three lines), and closes with a single line or couplet.

The poem can be written to any length and in any metrical pattern, although iambic pentameter is most frequently used in English. A fourteen-line version may be referred to as a terza rima sonnet. The rhyme scheme is a b a, b c b, c d c, d e d, etc. ending y z y, z z or y z y, z.

Good Shepherd

Yes, I was there the night the heavens rang	a
with angel song and dazzled us below.	b
I heard each syllable the spirits sang,	a
and, yes, I heard them order us to go.	b
If I had gone, who would have watched the flock?	c
My favourite ewe was lame and pregnant, so	b
I had no wish to leave her. And the stock	c
is valuable. What if thieves should find	d
our beasts? I waited, heard the morning cock	c
crow distant sunrise. All at once my mind	d
swarmed with portentous murmurings of deep	e
betrayal. Was I wrong to stay behind?	d
No minute of that night was spent in sleep.	e
Good shepherd. I would die to save my sheep.	e

Villanelle

Originally a round song of the French countryside, the villanelle is a haunting form with regular refrains and only two rhymes through-out. It may be written in any single line length and metre, and consists of an odd number of tercets followed by a quatrain. The rhyming first and last lines of the stanza recur alternately as the closing line of each stanza, and together as a couplet at the end of the poem, while the second lines of all the stanzas rhyme with each other.

The rhyme pattern is A1 b A2, a b A1, a b A2, a b A1, a b A2, a b A1 A2.

Seascape

My son had never seen the sea before.	A1
I chose this perfect, heat stained August day.	b
He revelled in the treasures of the shore.	A2
He took delight in everything he saw,	a
and paddled in the ripples of the bay.	b
My son had never seen the sea before.	A1
He heard a seashell echo water's roar	a
and sifted sand from spade to bucket, play	b
he revelled in. The treasures of the shore,	A2
of seaweed, crab and driftwood made a store,	a
a hoard for home. I told him not to stray.	b
My son had never seen the sea before.	A1
I should have watched more carefully, made sure.	a
I should have known that he would creep away.	b
He revelled in the treasures of the shore.	A2
I knew, before they gave up looking for	a
my child, the breakers gorged themselves on prey.	b
My son had never seen the sea before.	A1
He revelled in the treasures of the shore.	A2

When composing a villanelle, always bear in mind the number of repeats of the first and third lines, and the fact that they will appear together to close the poem. It is perhaps easier to start from the couplet and work backwards, or there may be a risk of writing nonsense at the end of the poem. Contemporary villanelles allow some latitude with the refrains for variety and interest.

Petrarchan Sonnet
The Italian sonnet is named after the poet Petrarch. It consists of fourteen lines of iambic pentameter, with a turn between the octave (the eight lines that open the poem) and sestet (the final six lines). The octave sets out and develops the subject of the poem, and the sestet makes and carries through a shift in thought or some new perception.

The rhyme scheme of the octave is invariably a b b a a b b a, while the sestet may rhyme c d e c d e or c d c d c d.

The close repetition of the octave carries the bonus of the sound value of the third to sixth lines, where the b a a b pattern reflects and offsets the original a b b a.

Sea Dream

I walked beneath the sea in dreams last night.	a
I felt my feet fall, sinking in wet sand.	b
Fish single, shoaled, swam by me. I could stand	b
and breathe and speak, could see by cobalt light	a
weed ribbons, water fossilled wood bleached white.	a
Rock crops rough-fingered me, shells pearled my hand,	b
sea wrack bound up my hair, salt seared its brand	b
to burn me. Water weight pressed me to flight.	a
I woke in terror of the fantasy,	c
retched wavelets from my lungs, ripped from my hair	d
green strands, knew dread of gaping sunken caves.	e
And yet some siren drag of ecstasy	c
caught me, forced fear aside, wailed out, 'Beware –	d
your fate lurks, beckoning, below the waves.'	e

This rigid pattern has been adapted considerably, notably by Wordsworth, who practised unusual line groupings and different rhyme patterns in the sestet, and by Milton, who shunned the distinct break in mood between the octave and sestet.

Shakespearian Sonnet

The Italian sonnet was introduced into this country in the early fifteen hundreds, and the English or Shakespearian sonnet developed out of it. (Shakespeare was not its first, but arguably its most accomplished writer.) Italian vocabulary produces many more options in rhyming sounds than English, and so an English form evolved based on seven different rhymes rather than five.

The turn in the poem occurs much later than in the Italian form, after three quatrains, allowing a final couplet to sum up the poem, or produce some new insights. This abrupt closing of the poem contrasts with the more fluid, musical style of the Italian sestet. Iambic pentameter is still used, but the rhyme scheme now reads a b a b c d c d e f e f g g.

Blurred Image

I paint my pictures, place them on the floor,	a
my board and canvas covering cold tiles.	b
I nail my palette high behind the door,	a
compose my other self in mock-real smiles.	b
You burst into my room. Your footprints sink	c
impressions in the tar of paint, half-dried;	d
and as you shift your weight the imprints link	c
in chains which double, oozing squat and wide.	d
You lie across my pictures, find your ease	e
by moulding tints and textures into one	f
blurred image, change my colours as you please,	e
distort my shapes, blot out my skies, my sun.	f
I leave in silence, lock the door to find	g
a larger screen than I have left behind.	g

Spenser developed a chain-rhymed form of the English sonnet, with a rhyme scheme of a b a b b c b c c d c d e e. This, however, forfeits the advantage of the extra two rhyming sounds, and has never been popular.

Limerick

Moving from the sonnet to the limerick is perhaps travelling from the sublime to the ridiculous, from a beautiful lyric to the classic joke form. The five-line pattern which rhymes a a b b a is doubtless familiar to everybody in the nursery rhyme 'Hickory Dickory Dock.'

Nowadays limericks take slightly longer lines, using a basic metrical pattern of one iambus and two anapaests for each of the 'a' rhyming lines, and one iambus and one anapaest for the 'b' lines. A great deal of latitude is allowed.

A writer who hopes to be smart	a
Should take this advice to his heart.	a
Rejection is sad,	b
But it isn't as bad	b
As failing to practise his art.	a

Syllable count forms

As we saw in the previous chapter, it is possible to write a poem with no rhyme or regular metre, but using patterns in the number of syllables to provide a unity holding the poem together. These syllabic poems may still be singing and resonant.

Cinquain

An unrhymed American form, this was devised by the poet Adelaide Crapsey and, as its name suggests, has five lines (of predominantly iambic metre). The lines have two, four, six, eight and two syllables respectively.

> I see
> a shadow on
> my mirror, looking past
> reflection, warning winter comes –
> my ghost.

Haiku
Perhaps the most widely used Japanese syllabic form, this tercet has five syllables in its first line, seven in its second and five in its third.

Regardless of its tightness of form, a haiku sets out to examine something of the universe. It should encapsulate an element of a season and evoke a mood. Its final line should provide some comment or reflection on the first two lines, but it should be open ended, implying a continuity of thought.

> Robins burn scarlet
> against monochrome of frost –
> exhorting the sun.

Clogyrnach
This is one of many Welsh syllabic forms which rely on syllable count and rhyme (often with midline rhymes). It has six lines of eight, eight, five, five, three and three syllables, although the final six syllables may be written as one line. The rhyme scheme is a a b b b a.

Christmas trees are fascinating	a
for a kitten, crouched and waiting	a
to pounce. She pulls claws,	b
pats mischievous paws,	b
frees baubles,	(slant) b
starts chasing.	a

The clogyrnach may be used as the stanza pattern for a poem of any length.

Calligramme and concrete

For these forms to work fully, they must be seen rather than just heard. A calligramme is a poem written in a particular shape, making use of the block of print or the areas of space to reinforce the message of the poem. 'Easter Wings' by George Herbert is a good example.

Where calligramme indicates shape, concrete poetry is ideogrammic. It is printed in such a way that the eye perceives a picture reinforced by the words.

```
say when say when
say when say when say when p
say when say when          o
                           u
                           r
                           p
                           o
                           u
                           r
                           p
                           o
                           u
                           r
                             when
                             when
                             when
```

These poems are fun to write and tax the imagination – and the versatility of the typewriter. Some excellent examples of the form are by American poet May Swenson.

If forms fascinate you, do consult the specialised books which list hundreds more than space permits here. It is immensely rewarding to discover for yourself the dynamics of pattern that have so inspired generations of poets in the past, and continue to inspire contemporary writers.

Exercises

16 Browse through the forms described in this chapter and go back to the lines written in Exercise 9 and developed in Exercise 15. Experiment, putting the lines into different forms. Does any form seem particularly appropriate as a medium for these lines?

17 Write two Chaucerian roundels, one in strict metre and the other with no metrical restrictions. Which do you prefer?

18 Try writing couplets on various subjects which could form the refrains of a villanelle. If any couplet strikes you as being especially interesting, write the complete poem.

19 Write some limericks by way of relaxation – humorous ones about your friends, and abusive ones about your enemies. This is excellent therapy. (If you must, change the names to protect the guilty.)

20 Produce a concrete poem using food as a theme.

21 Try to find some pictures of landscapes in particular seasons (a calendar may be a good source of these). Write about what you see in haiku and in sonnet form. Which paints the more interesting picture?

7

WHILE YOU WRITE . . .

We have spent some time considering ideas, vocabulary, rhythm, metre, rhyme, and form. After you have made your choices about these elements of a poem and started to write, there are various points you should still bear firmly in mind.

First, you are writing a whole poem. The poem does not consist only of rhyme or of vocabulary. All the elements are going to fuse into a harmonious whole if the poem is to work. During the process of putting words on to paper, it may be best to forget each, separate subject. Take the wide view, and visualise the poem as a whole at all times.

Only when things seem to be going wrong will you need to analyse each aspect of your piece in depth. While the poem is humming along, do not question it. Pour your words out on to paper. Let your instinct take over. The time for revision comes later.

So how does the poem start to hum? Unfortunately there is no easy or direct answer to this, partly because the 'excitement' element of each poet – and of each poem produced – is unique. No matter how carefully you try to define the approach to setting words down, you will always come up against a vagueness in the mind which is the magical part of the creative process.

Finding a form

From my own experience, nothing ever starts to happen in a poem until words begin to appear on the paper. The first words may well be gibberish. Sometimes I write the date, and my name, my address, a few lines of someone else's poem . . . anything to encourage the pen to pass over the paper.

Sooner or later my mind disciplines my hand into writing

words for the poem. There may be just one or two words, or a number of phrases. There may be a complete line or more. At this very early stage the form the poem will take may begin to emerge.

The words may have a predominantly iambic metre. If so, I start to manipulate them into lines of four or five iambic feet, or into free verse with an emphasis on an iambic pattern. They may have a staccato feel about them. Then I set them down in the form of short lines to be compatible with the sharp sound. They may not, of course, offer the slightest indication of any emerging form, so I simply set down each word and phrase that comes into my head, using a new line for each idea.

The new lines on the paper are important. If you are going to write poetry rather than prose, you must think in line formation from the start. A piece which has its roots as a continuous prose passage and ends up as a poem will always make you feel that it has been forced into a 'container' of the wrong shape.

As soon as you begin feeling your way into a particular form, you are setting yourself a framework in which to write. Your words are no longer random and chaotic. They are fitting into a pattern which may be as tightly structured as a villanelle or as loose as a piece of free verse. The framework is the skeleton to be fleshed out with your words. Keep them within its framework, and you will not have to expend your precious creative energy worrying about shape – the form gives your poem its shape.

Remember that your first ideas about form may not be the best, and when you come to the revision process you may wish to change the whole pattern of your poem. But for the time being you need that framework of form, so use its discipline as a vehicle for your idea.

Free verse is not the option to select if no set form occurs to you. The decision to write in free verse should be taken positively, as the best possible medium in which to express yourself. A negative use of free verse chosen because nothing else seems right is likely to produce a weak poem.

If you have an idea which begs to be written in poetry but does not suggest any particular form to you, it could be that you are not yet ready to write that poem. Retain the ideas for it in note form and leave the topic alone for a while. The chances are you will return to it and find that a form does present itself to you after all. I have twice had the experience of wanting to write a particular poem without knowing which form it should take – simply because of my own lack of knowledge. On each occasion I read of a previously untried form and knew at once that it was the right vehicle for the idea. Both of the resulting poems have since been published.

Quite simply, do not strain after form. Allow the creative process that urges you to write poetry to guide you into the best pattern for each poem you produce. When you trust this instinct, it will usually serve you well.

Subject material

No matter how strongly you feel about the subject material of your poem, remember your line of approach may change while you are writing it down. Never question this when it happens. Just make sure that you keep a record of all the ideas that flit through your mind in relation to your subject, whether or not they seem relevant to this poem. There may be further writing to come out of the topic when you have finished working on the current piece.

The actual writing process is different for every writer. The same writer may use different techniques, depending on the poem being produced. In the simplest possible terms, there are three fundamental ways of setting down the material you wish to cover.

No matter how many notes you made in the preparation stages of your poem, you may wish to write out a new series of highly detailed notes to cover all the ideas you intend to include. As we have already considered, this approach is especially helpful if you are in doubt about form.

You may prefer to launch directly into your poem without such notes and get all your ideas down on paper as quickly as possible before you even glance back to see what you have written.

You may find that you want to launch directly into the poem, but amend and alter it as you write, making each line fit your requirements of content, rhythm, rhyme and metre before you move on to the next.

I find that this last technique is the one I use most frequently, but it should be stressed that every poem is a new adventure, and may need an unfamiliar line of approach.

However you choose your form and select your manner of dealing with subject material, keep remembering that the poem you are creating is uniquely yours. Its success will depend on the fusion of all the elements we have covered in earlier chapters, and on the vital spark that kindles it to life, where you take a great leap of the imagination and let your poem soar freely.

Are you sitting comfortably?

Make yourself as comfortable as you can when you write. If you are happiest at a typewriter in an office-style environment, create this within your home. If you like to curl up in an armchair with an exercise book on your knee, do that. Write when you are alone in the house if you need peace, or with the television on, or family present if you need noise.

Your eccentricities of writing are not affectations. They are not whims but an important part of the total process. Experiment by writing in different places at different times of day to find your most successful way of working. When you have found it, insist on adopting it.

I believe poetry can only be written with a black biro in an exercise book when you lie down on your stomach on the living-room floor, preferably too close to the fire. It is a solitary activity which can take place any time between the second mug of coffee of the day and five in the afternoon, or between ten at night and two in the morning. Poetry written outside those hours or in blue ink is destined to fail.

If this suggestion confirms your worst fears . . . so be it. It hurts nobody, does not frighten the horses, and gives me a psychological boost. When conditions fit into the pattern I have described, I start writing in the belief that I can produce something useful, possibly even something good. This does not prevent me from writing rubbish, but makes me write in a pleasantly optimistic frame of mind.

66

Make a list of your own rules. They are probably just as silly – but if they work, do not question them.

The first draft

If you can, get a complete first draft of your poem on to paper at one sitting. No matter how hard you try, you will never again be able to reproduce the identical circumstances of the moment you started to write. Your mood, the light in the room, your position, the thoughts flitting through your brain all contribute to the poem you are creating. By changing any one of these, you are altering the circumstances most conducive to production of that particular poem and interrupting the flow.

Poets have an advantage here over other writers. It would be impossible to write a novel at a single sitting, and difficult to produce a feature or short story in one go. Unless you are writing an epic, it is usually easy enough to get down on paper all the words that encompass your idea, or at least all the detailed notes for them. They may not appear in the best order or form for that particular poem. You will almost certainly alter some of them in the course of time, but the impetus that sparked the poem has been captured for ever and no amount of alteration can change that.

Fixing the mind

Concentrate fully on your poem while you write. Fix your mind firmly on the thoughts you are putting on to paper. Writing poetry is all about concentration. You are condensing an idea and distilling it into an essence that will convey your message most effectively. You are also directing all of your attention into the piece you are producing. Ignore the telephone, the door, demands of other people in the house. Focus every fibre of your being on the page.

If your attention begins to wander, ask yourself why. It could be that your mind cannot cope with the sheer weight of your task, and needs to break away and drift for a little while into the realms of non-poetry trivia. If this is the case spare a few minutes to consider international politics or what you will have for tea, and then bring it back to its important considerations.

If the reason for wandering is a loss of interest in the poem, or a sense of boredom with it, start to question your work carefully. After all, if the poem bores its writer before it is finished, how much more boring will the completed version seem to the reader?

Enjoy the writing

Ask yourself continually whether you are actively enjoying the creation of your poem. Even a piece that disturbs or distresses you should engender pride and pleasure as you write it. When I am actually writing a poem I am gripped by the excitement of the experience. My heart beats faster. All my senses are heightened. Time passes unnoticed. The quality of the work being produced does not matter. At that moment, the naked power of creation holds me, and I am in step with the world.

I feel that the poem should force itself to be written; you should not be forcing yourself to write. I do not believe that poetry produced out of some perverse sense of duty will work on any other than a superficial level. In saying this, I am not denying the value of writing as an exercise. But whether you write from exercise or inspiration, the need to write must be burning within you, and will only be satisfied while you are putting words on to paper.

Know that poetry is a power source. Its strength is frightening as it grips you and, later, your readers. If its grip is slack, it may need considerable rethinking.

In short, never be half-hearted about poetry. A wishy-washy reaction on your part will communicate itself to your reader. Let your writing be a way of life, not an uncomfortable by-product of an interest in literature.

Do not try to be too clever in your writing. Obscure images and vocabulary propelling half your readers to the dictionary do not infer your erudition. They are signs of a muddled mind and guaranteed to infuriate rather than impress.

Always write with precision. Precise handling of thoughts and images will result in a poem whose meaning shines out through strong, plain words. Clumsy handling of ideas leads only to a chaotic end product.

Remember to be specific in all things rather than general. 'It was a cold, rainy day in early spring' is a dull generalisation. 'Snowdrops dripped and shivered' puts across the same idea but creates a highly specific picture.

Be aware of the way your own poetry can move you, just as you can be moved by the poetry of others. It is not an affectation to laugh or weep aloud as you write – it is an indication that the poem is working.

While you are at the stage of continually reading back over the words you have written, do not forget to read aloud from time to time. Your words work on a whole new level when you hear them spoken out.

Write with fidelity to your idea, but never forget that you must write with passion. A fierce outflow of emotion should not be stemmed. It is the strength of your work.

Whether you are producing a world-changing epic or a little uncomplimentary verse for your best friend's fortieth birthday card, write to the very best of your ability. A poet who cares about his writing should be able to produce a competent piece of work every time he sits down to write. Any offering which falls short of competence weakens his status in his own eyes, and in the eyes of his readers.

At the other end of the scale, you may be aware that your poem is not merely competent but has a touch of brilliance. Do not let false modesty prevent you from acknowledging this to yourself. While it may be arrogant to tell the world that your work is wonderful, it is honest to admit the truth of it to yourself. Every now and again you are likely to produce a masterpiece. These never occur as frequently as we might wish, but when they do come they make sense of the whole crazy process of writing. So we should not underestimate them.

The title

While actually writing the poem, keep an area of your mind on the lookout for a suitable title. Some people need a title before they can begin to write. I cannot put down a single phrase without a heading at the top, but I always regard that as a 'working title', certain in the knowledge that it will be changed at least once before the poem moves from notebook to type.

Titles are important, and may take longer to produce than the rest of the poem. The title is the handle by which readers will grasp your piece. An untitled poem becomes known by its first line, or is referred to as 'Poem', or given a number. (Shakespeare seems to have limited his exploration of titles to the plays; his sonnets are invariably and unimaginatively known by numbers.)

Your title should be precise and challenging. It should tempt the reader in. You should select it with the care a publisher lavishes on the jacket of a book. The casual browser is unlikely to be hooked unless it is dramatic and eyecatching. Imagine a reader running his finger down the contents list of a poetry book or magazine. Which titles will encourage him to read further?

My own titles give me no end of problems. I can usually come up with something satisfactory, but seldom feel completely happy with my choice. The obvious title is dull, and the less obvious runs the risk of being obscure. My favourite titles were all suggested by other people, and offered spontaneously after first reading or hearing the poem. I had laboured for ages in most cases and produced nothing of worth.

If you have trouble with titles, collect lists of poetry competition winners and short-listed pieces. You may be sure that the writers have worked hard on the titles of these. Without considering the actual poems, ask yourself how you feel about their names. See if any of them inspire you to think of something more imaginative for one of your own poems.

Pitfalls

As you write, watch out for your own acknowledged weaknesses and try to avoid them. For example, I have a tendency to make lists where one or two phrases would suffice, and I overuse the definite article. I overdescribe and repeat myself – fatal in the tight confines of a poem. So each time I put pen to paper, I chant a little catechism of my failings and circle or cross out offending areas of text.

At the same time, bear in mind your intentions for your poem when you set out to write it. Quite simply, are you still writing the poem you planned to put down on paper?

If the answer is yes, there is no problem. If it is no, there may still be no problem. There is nothing to prevent you from following this new course and going back to your original idea some other time, or even abandoning the original idea in favour of something better.

More important than the question about your first intentions for the poem is the more general question: does this poem have something to say? You should ask yourself this continually during the writing process. For a poem which has nothing to communicate has little reason to exist and none to be read. No matter how slight the message, there should be something there to interest the reader. A piece with no message at all is not likely to interest a reader in any case, as it will fail to impress the editor selecting material to be published.

My final suggestion to consider while writing may seem a strange one in the light of all the others. It is just this: be careful not to take yourself too seriously. Poets run no more risk of becoming pompous and self-important than anyone else. But in a poet it shows through and weakens the work. Laugh at yourself, write a few frivolous, fun pieces and read William McGonagall.

Exercises

22 Go back to any poem you have produced in the past and analyse the thought processes that went into its first draft. Do you recall any fragments of an idea that were unused in the end? If so, could they appear in another poem?

23 Allow yourself a spell of gazing into the middle distance and thinking about titles. Are you happy with the ones you have used in the past? Can you think of any better ones? Can you think of a title to which you would like to write a poem?

24 Spend a few minutes reading aloud from the poetry of other people. Then read the same poems through silently. Which had more effect on you? Which approach was more enjoyable? Did either form of reading open new insights which the other did not?

8

REVISION

When the first draft of your poem is safely down on paper the business of revision begins. Some writers find this a stimulating and rewarding process. For others it is a chore. Whether you enjoy it or not, it is necessary.

It is difficult to be objective about your own work at the best of times, but when you have only just finished writing a piece it is almost impossible. Depending on your usual reaction to your work, you may feel elated or immeasurably depressed. In either case you should wait for a while – a few hours, days or even weeks – before you start to revise. Distance lends a sort of objectivity. It is much easier to be self-critical when you have forgotten how long it took you to write the poem, and how you agonised over its creation. Much of the revision process depends on cutting your poem, scoring out every word and phrase you can delete. It is very important to remember to try to think of this as 'pruning' rather than 'cutting'. Pruning is an activity essential to the health of your piece as a whole, and is an artistic and creative act.

While you are revising, bear in mind that you are putting the finishing touches to a poem which may be around in collections and anthologies for centuries to come. The work you put in now could be appreciated for generations. By the law of averages this is unlikely to happen, but you need the grain of hope to keep yourself working with optimism.

Listening to the words

Start by reading your poem aloud, slowly and clearly, just as though you were reading it to an audience. Listen carefully to your own words. Your immediate response may be one of surprise that the poem is so effective. It may produce a frisson of excitement for you. You may think to yourself, 'This is exactly what I wanted to say'. If you react in this way, you could have produced a winner, but it still makes sense to go on with the revision process. There are few poems which cannot be improved.

It is more likely that your own response will be a little less effusive. If that is the case, ask yourself three simple questions about your poem. Does it make sense? Are you comfortable with the reading? Does the poem have some sort of message to communicate, whether slight or highly significant? If the answer to any of these questions is no, there is a fundamental problem with the poem.

This does not make your poem a candidate for the waste paper basket, but it does mean that you should look at it very carefully and decide whether you wish to persevere with it. If you do, then make sure you are severe in all your criticisms of it. It is already a poem with problems, and you need to iron them all out meticulously if you are to create a good poem out of your revision.

If you decide not to continue with it, do not throw it away. Keep it in a special file full of 'failed' poems, and every now and again take your file and allow yourself a 'bring out your dead' writing session.

This involves looking through all the failed work you have produced and extracting from it interesting lines or phrases, ideas that might work in a different form, good rhymes, strong images, telling metaphors – anything that could be recycled and used in a new poem. Keep all these useful extracts in your poetry notebook for future reference.

If you feel that your poem does contain a message, ask yourself whether it is the theme you intended to communicate. If it is, well and good. If it is not, do not worry. You can always write another poem to convey your original message, and you have the 'by-product' of the poem carrying the new message. .

The detailed analysis

Overall effect
Moving away from the general effectiveness of your poem, examine every aspect of it in detail.

Does your piece contain the right amount of material? This may seem a silly question, but the delicate balance which is part of the communication of poetry will be thrown out if you have tried to stuff your work with an excess of subject matter.

You may be trying to express a number of different ideas in one poem, when each should have had its own poem. You may have used too many examples, or included too much explanation of your theme. If any of these is the case, cut drastically. Keep cutting extraneous ideas, words, phrases and whole lines out of the poem until you have pared it to the bone. You will reach a stage where it has been so abbreviated that it no longer makes sense. At that stage flesh out your bones, but using only your lean meat to do so. Do not discard the 'fat', but store it in your 'bring out your dead' file.

If, on the other hand, your poem does not contain enough material, it will be too slight to intrigue or entertain a reader. Check that you have not reduced the essence of your writing into such a tight form that it is too condensed, and ceases to make sense without further explanation. Consider whether you could elaborate on the text without producing a piece which appears to be artificially padded. Ask yourself whether new, associated ideas would fit into your poem.

Does it begin and end in the right place? It is tempting to explain your setting before the meat of the poem is introduced. A poem is too short a vehicle to sustain this device. An overstated ending is an anticlimax, and insults the intelligence of your reader. If your poem was written with clarity, he does not need this explanation.

The pattern
Look at the pattern of your words on the page. If your only copy of the poem is handwritten, make a typed copy. They look different. But do remember after you have typed the poem that it is not fixed simply because you can see it in print.

Ask whether the shape is pleasing and appropriate for the subject matter. Have you used free verse, a set form, a syllable count? If in doubt about the shell of the poem, experiment with it. Try writing just a few lines in a different form or using different line lengths. If any of these experiments seems to fit your poem, produce the whole idea in this form. You can always go back to your original if you prefer, but you will get a much clearer idea of how well your poem works if you have something against which to compare it.

Line structure

When the shape of the poem seems right, look at it line by line with particular reference to the endings. If you have used punctuation at the end of a line, is it correct? Where you are unsure of punctuation, check in any English grammar book. If there is no written punctuation, remember that the enjambement implies the merest hint of a pause before the reader's eye moves to the next line. Do these subtle pauses make sense? Or are there more appropriate places to break from one line to the next? If your poem is in free verse, question the line pattern most carefully. (A set form poem offers its writer a little more help with line structure.) Have you used powerful words at the end of the line, its strongest point? Weaker and less significant words fit more naturally at the beginning of the next line.

Rhyme, rhythm and metre

Have you used either full or slant rhyme? Is there a unity in your use of rhyme? A rhymed poem which changes its expected pattern half way dissatisfies the reader. An otherwise unrhymed poem which suddenly moves into rhyme for no apparent reason is similarly unsatisfying. Remember that there is a world of difference between a slight shift in the use of rhyme for the artistry of the piece and a breakdown caused by slack writing.

Has the meaning of a line ever been sacrificed in order to manipulate a rhyme? If it has, you are making a nonsense of your whole work. Reconstruct your lines until the meaning and the rhyme scheme flow along together comfortably.

Look at the rhythm and metre. Does your sound stress pattern work with your poem or against it? Are any breaks in the rhythm there to create a particular effect, or again a result of clumsy handling?

The alterations needed to correct rhyme, rhythm and metre may seem excessive and tedious. But remember that the hardest part of writing a poem is the translation of your fundamental idea into the words and images through which it is communicated. The comparatively easy work of tidying your words into their best possible combinations should not be shirked.

Word choice
Consider your vocabulary. Have you used the best possible word to convey your meaning at every point? Is there an unnecessary word anywhere? There is no room for a wasted word in a poem. Have you used any unintentional repetitions of word or of sound? Even the smallest word draws attention to itself in the poem's tight construction. Repetitions of 'and', 'in', 'of' or 'the' will glare at a reader. Make sure there are no inappropriate rhymes which appear merely because of the pronunciation of the language. If there are any you did not spot during the writing process, change them.

The whole poem

When you have analysed its constituent parts in detail and made appropriate revisions, take the long view of your poem once again. Does it speak in your voice? This is a difficult question to answer. Establishing an individual style is the aim of every poet. It can only be reached through experience. You cannot cultivate a style without actually writing. And once it has been established, you must take care not to parody your own manner, resorting to weak writing in a style which has proved successful for you in the past.

Ask yourself whether anything about your poem makes you cringe as you read it. Be honest. If the answer is yes, you will cringe even more when you see your name against the work in print, should it ever reach that stage.

Run through a checklist of your own weaknesses, even though you were considering them throughout the writing of your poem. Again it helps to be brutally honest with yourself. If you know you have a tendency to invert expressions for the sake of rhyme, or that metre gives you problems, look once more at those facets of your poem.

Now look at your favourite parts of your poem, the words and phrases which please you the most. Question them very carefully. Arthur Quiller-Couch offered the advice 'murder your darlings' to student Alistair Cooke, and it remains good advice. Be sure that everything you have included is there for the sake of your poem, and not because you think it sounds good. (Your 'darlings' may have a by-product, in that they might provide you with a good title.)

Ask yourself three more questions. Is your poem special? Does it offer new insights, shed new light on your subject, or approach a well-tried subject with freshness? Does it fascinate its reader?

You will realise that these are the most difficult questions to answer for yourself. This is where a 'first reader' becomes your best help.

Your first reader

Ideally this is not a member of your family, who is likely to be either hypercritical or over enthusiastic about everything you produce. It should be another practising poet, whose work you admire and whose honest criticism you respect. First reading should be a mutual act, each sharpening his critical faculties on the other's work, and each gaining a useful reaction to his own work.

Your first reader looks at your poem with two advantages. He is distanced from the actual work involved in writing, and has no special affection for particular areas of the poem. Also he is ignorant of the thought processes that created it, and can tell whether it works without the background knowledge of its creator.

However deeply you trust your first reader's opinion, do not automatically accept everything he says. Rather have another look at your poem armed with the advice you have been offered, and decide whether you should accept or reject that advice.

The final stages

At the end of the day the poem will bear your name. Repeat the revision process as often as you wish – allowing time to elapse between each revision – and seek as many opinions of your work as you need. (As well as a first reader, you may like to consult a writing class or circle, a postal advice service, or other poets of your acquaintance.) When you are completely happy with your work, leave it alone. You may feel that you will never be a hundred per cent satisfied, but you owe it to readers of your poetry to present them with a finished copy.

Poets frequently alter poems after publication, and later versions of them appear in different collections. This may, of course, indicate that they were inadequately revised in the first place. Or it may be that a maturing approach to poetry makes them aware of flaws in earlier work. Altering a recently published piece only leads to confusion, and vague feelings of dissatisfaction in the readers. Changing a poem written twenty years before denies the growth process which moulded the writer of today.

Having made this point, I should confess that some of my own poems have been published in more than one version. I am not wholly happy about this, but in each case felt it was better to amend a recent poem than to let it be reprinted without certain improvements. In other words, I should have spent more time on revision before first publication.

The business of revision is clinical. It involves analysis, logic and brainwork. The creation of poetry is a more mystical activity, with instinct, with half-formed ideas springing from deep inside your consciousness, and gut reaction. While revision should iron out the flaws in your work, it should never erase the magic. It is possible to make your poem bland, or even to kill it by over-revision. However many times you rewrite, you should not lose the frisson, the inherent excitement in the response to your poem.

79

Exercises

25 Go back to any poem you have written and apply revision techniques to it. Put the original and the revised copy away for a few days, Look at them again, and decide which is better.

26 Consider any two contemporary poems (other than your own), one in free verse, the other in set form. Can you see any areas which might have gained from revision? Which would you have altered more extensively, the free verse or the set form poem?

9

TWO POEMS – START TO FINISH

We have considered various aspects of the craft of writing poetry in general terms. Perhaps it is now a good idea to move away from the general and into the specific. This chapter deals with two poems from start to finish, one in free verse, the other in set form.

Free verse poem

Initial idea
The poem began on the level of a simple exercise. Using suggestion no. 6 in the 'Finding the Idea' section of Chapter 2, I opened my dictionary at random, closed my eyes and pointed to a word. It was 'drooping'. It occurred within a definition, but was not the word being defined. I did not want to lead my thoughts into any particular direction, so I purposely avoided reading around the word and do not know in which definition it appeared.

I wrote down 'drooping' and allowed myself two minutes by the (doubtless inaccurate) kitchen timer to pour out all the words I thought of, regardless of what they were. The resulting page reads:

Drooping
sad
wilting
flowers
flesh
hanging
pendulum
broken stem
ailing
depressed

> tired
> overworked
> drifting towards sleep
> failing
> falling
> dead flower
> single flower in bedroom
> turning brown – stiff – sepia

Perhaps an analyst could make some pronouncement about my level of sanity from all this. The poet took over from the mechanic within the final ten seconds of the two minutes, with the phrase 'dead flower'.

Writing this led directly to the next two phrases, for which a little explanation is required. At the time when I set myself the exercise, my elder daughter had recently moved out of the family home and into her own flat. Her room was to be refurnished for her own use in the future or as a guest room. As we moved things around we found a single dead flower on the carpet, the last reminder of a bouquet presented by a former boyfriend some months before. Her younger sister placed the dead flower in a glass and left it beside the hand basin, where it remained for no good reason other than the fact that nobody moved it while the room was redecorated and refurnished.

This single flower became a focal point of the room and was not actually moved until guests were about to stay in there. Its owner, meanwhile, was delighted that the flower had been found and said she would like it to be kept.

If you have not yet given up out of boredom, the point of this explanation is that I commented to myself when this happened that there might be a poem to come. I did not think any more about it on a conscious level until the word 'drooping' recalled the dead flower.

All at once I wanted to communicate a sense of .the way in which an unimportant, tangible thing can be the fixing point for deep emotion. Hence the flower embodied parental love for a child, reactions to the child's growing into a woman, letting go of the young person who was going to try independence, and the unbreakable link that would remain.

Now that the word list had dredged up an idea for a poem, it was time to take the development a stage further.

The next brief set of notes was written about ten minutes later, and without any time constraint. It allowed me to explore my half-formed ideas and put them into some sort of order. Although I frequently produce work in complete lines at an early stage, I find it useful to develop lists when there are various ideas buzzing around in my mind. While they are still in my head, they are muddled. By harnessing them to paper, I can begin to develop them and change their order. This list reads:

Fresh flowers – promise, youth, beauty
Stems and petals turning hard and crisp – experience
Why keep one flower?
Moving on – leaving flower behind
Texture of paper
No smell
Nostalgia
Flower found and rescued
Dead flower placed in glass
Room empty except for flower
Flower takes over to fill the room and the imagination
Need to leave the flower there as a link
Conversion of room into a guest bedroom
Keeping flower in cupboard under the hand basin

The only word which is not directly related to the poem I was intending to write is 'nostalgia'. This is not a suggestion but a warning; a warning that the poem could easily become over sentimental and mawkish, which must be avoided at all costs.

First draft

Two or three days passed before I felt ready to tackle a first draft of the poem. I began to write when I knew I had an hour available for the work, which would certainly offer enough time for me to get a first draft on to paper in one sitting. This is the initial version complete with comments made at the time and given here in brackets:

Working title – **One Flower** – (definitely wrong)

Your/her/the room is empty . . . ('your' most intimate?)
No clutter covers shelves and floor.
Posters are gone. Blu tack scars
walls where your favourite stars smiled.
Four blobs of dust/dust rings surround
imprints/impressions/ruts in the carpet
where your bed stood. Your soap
has dried and cracked. cobwebs
mist cling/reach from book to book.   (clumsy)

You have moved on,
drawn from home and school
to work and independence.   (ugh)
Your room holds just a trace scent
of your perfume, and on the floor
one flower.   (mentioned too late)

This flower breathed
its part in your first bouquet -
first flower from first true love.
Its first blush faded long ago,
aged pink to sepia,
fleshed carnation crisping to parchment. (too wordy)
Its stem is string flaked,
neck (biological term?) a husked cup.

No accident left this one flower behind   (iambic pentameter)
when all the rest were binned.
Perhaps this is your link,
your moment's reaching into yesterday.   (iambic
                                            pentameter)

Perhaps more care placed this
than fixed/arranged its fellows in their vase.
Your flower, unscented now, stands in a glass,   (iambic
                                                  pentameter)

84

pervades the air.   (wrong)

In time to come, your room
no longer yours but newly part
of our old house, will change.
New furniture and carpets
will welcome guests,
unlittered by your life.

This flower will have no place
beside the basin; I shall hide it safe   (iambic pentameter)
behind the store of soap and towels.
A talisman/amulet/charm/memento of your growing up,
it closes tight the/our link, new cord
between us, symbol to set us free.

I knew before I started that the title was wrong, and was purely a
working 'handle' for the poem. The first question was one viewpoint. I wanted to tell the tale from my own angle, and had to
choose in the first word between addressing my daughter directly
(you) or indirectly (she), or distancing the experience from the personalities involved (the). By line four this problem had resolved
itself. The poem told me to use the most direct approach when I
found myself writing 'your' without thinking about it.

　　Some words and phrases were destined to be altered the
moment they were written. I knew at once that they were wrong.
Other words cried out for special attention, because they were
repeated inappropriately, glared because they were my 'weakness'
words (such as 'the') or simply did not look right. (I wanted to
put something on to paper, even if it proved to be quite wrong,
rather than leave any gaps in the draft.)

　　Sometimes alternative words are suggested, when more than one
idea presented itself at a time. I noted words showing an obvious
similarity of sound (e.g. 'stars'/'scars', 'behind'/'binned'). I checked
for other features of poetry (e.g. repetition of 'book', unscheduled
appearance of iambic pentameter). This was simply done as it
occurred to me during the first draft, so that I could bear such
devices in mind when working on revised versions.

85

There are a few words written alongside the text to state my initial impressions as the work was unfolding. 'Ugh' and 'clumsy' are, incidentally, somewhat restrained comments. A poem which presents more problems is likely to have more four-letter Anglo-Saxon words in the margin.

This first draft gave no difficulties with regard to form. The moment I started to write, the first few lines presented themselves in free verse, and that established itself as a comfortable, appropriate style for the whole poem. It felt casual and conversational. Stanza breaks appeared equally naturally, even though I realised from the start that the second, third and fourth stanzas would need a great deal of condensing.

The last two stanzas were produced more quickly. For one thing, I was beginning to tire. This was not, I felt, a case of becoming bored with the poem I was writing. It was due to the intensity of thought that was going into the draft, with mental exertion leading into physical exhaustion. The second reason was that pressure of time was greater than I thought. I had an appointment to attend and found that the hour allocated for the work had not, after all, been enough.

The last three lines of the poem were scribbled without much thought in just a few seconds, but I knew as I wrote them that I was coming close to the central message I was trying to communicate.

Throughout the writing I was aware that the poem taking shape under the pen was not a world-changer, but it was not going to be the worst thing I had ever produced. There was no sign of a good title and there were repetitions and heavy descriptions, but there was a kernel of truth that was worth developing.

At the end of the first draft I read the work aloud for the last time and put the pages away for a few days.

Revision

Less than a week later, reading the poem aloud, I was struck by its length, and realised it would need drastic cutting. The third and fourth stanzas were choked with unnecessary explanation. I was reasonably happy with the way my intended message communicated itself. I wanted to develop the piece.

I asked myself whether the poem started in the right place and knew at once that the first line was not required. The first stanza shows that the once-used room is empty. There is no need to tell that fact in the opening statement.

I did not, at that stage, type the poem, as I thought that the pattern on the page was unlikely to pose too many problems. There would be alterations to make in line structure, but they could be considered along with other facets of the poem.

I only noticed one instance of fully rhyming words placed close together, in the 'scars'/'stars' of the first stanza. Although unintentional, the effect was pleasing, so I left it.

Full repetition occurred in 'book to book' (first stanza), four uses of the word 'first' (third stanza) and overuse of 'the' (final stanza).

Slant rhyme was present in 'husked'/'cup' and 'behind'/'binned'. (At the time of producing the first draft and at the first reading of the revision process, I was not aware of any other instances of slant rhyme, although there proved to be several.)

I liked the full and slant rhyme, none of which seemed forced, but the full repetition was overdone.

Reading the work aloud had given the impression of a suitable flow in the rhythm, and there was no intended metre to consider. There were, however, those lines of unintentional iambic pentameter, which appeared three times in the eight lines of the fourth stanza.

The biggest question marks in the matter of vocabulary hung over the dust marks on the carpet, the cobwebs at the end of the first stanza, 'neck' at the end of the third stanza, the clichéd phrase 'pervades the air', the juxtaposition of 'newly' and 'old', and the correct description of the flower's function in the final lines.

Having highlighted some problem areas, and knowing that others would come to light when I started to work, I decided it was time to produce a second draft – still lacking an appropriate title. I ended up with this:

Second draft – untitled

No clutter covers shelves and floor.
Blu tack scars walls where your stars smiled.

Four dust rings mark the carpet
where your bed stood. Your soap
has dried out, cracked. Cobwebs
mist cling your books. The room holds just
trace scent of your perfume,
and on the floor
one flower.

These petals breathed their part
in first bouquet from first real love.
Blush faded long ago, aged
from pink to sepia.
Fresh carnation parchment crisped,
string stemmed/stem turned to string, neck a husked
cup.   (too much description)

No accident left this behind
when all the rest were binned.
You moved on, left your link
precision placed.
OR You moved on, precision placed your link.
Unscented now, your flower
stands in a glass, flavours
the air.

In time to come this room once yours
will change; new furniture and carpets
welcome guests, unlittered by your life/living here.
Your flower will not belong
and yet
I shall hide it, safe
beside/behind stored soap and towels.
An amulet that charmed your growing up,
it closes tight our link/links our chain,
new cord to bind us,
key to set us free.

In the first stanza, the poem seemed to work without the tautology of the first line. 'Favourite' was out. It was not only unnecessary, as the reader would infer that posters of film or pop stars on the walls would be of favourite characters, but also it seemed to blunt the effect of the full rhyme. I liked the idea of 'Blu tack'. It fixed the poem clearly into a time scale, as just one generation earlier would have used drawing pins or sticky tape. The clumsy 'surround ruts in the carpet' was simplified to 'mark the carpet', giving the unexpected bonus of a sound link: mark/tack. Regardless of my loss of credibility as a housewife, I wanted those cobwebs. Although I had not yet decided how to describe them, I managed to get rid of the ugly 'book to book'.

The second stanza was giving problems even as I wrote the first draft. I decided I was guilty of overstatement once again, and simply cut its first three lines. I hoped that the rest of the poem would show the situation and that I did not need to tell it in such a heavy-handed way. I was pleased to be able to introduce the flower earlier in the poem, at the strong point right at the end of the first stanza.

The new second stanza uses 'petals' at the beginning instead of repeating 'flower'. As well as avoiding repetition at that point I wanted to introduce a plural noun instead of a singular one. 'Its part in first bouquet' sounded clumsy – 'their' seemed better. I felt that a single repetition of 'first' worked poetically, and found it easy to omit the others. 'Real' replaced 'true' with 'love' to get rid of the cliché. 'Parchment crisped' enabled me to drop the second 'to'. I was still not sure how to describe the brittle filaments of the stem, but decided that the flower should have a 'neck', regardless of any botanical inaccuracy. I liked its sound against 'husked cup', which in turn seemed to be an accurate description.

I was unhappy with the weight of iambic pentameter and shortened those lines considerably in the revised version. I decided to remove the speculative repetition of 'perhaps' feeling that the motives alluded to had no place within this poem and might cloud its intended message. Instead of leaving room for doubt, I allowed my imagination to furnish the certainty of 'precision placed'. The end of the penultimate stanza merely tidies the word order and drops the expected 'pervades' for 'flavours', which picks up the sound of 'flower'

The 'newly/old' question resolved itself when I realised how clumsy those lines sounded, and that I could put across the same message in the two words, 'once yours', instead of ten.

The final stanza seemed to belong with the previous one. Its wordy opening was condensed to remove the clumsiness of 'beside the/behind the'. I decided to opt for 'amulet' to describe the flower. For some reason it conjured up images of antiquity in my mind and suggested dust and brittleness. As 'charm' was a close contender, it was allowed the consolation prize of appearing as a verb. It asked for 'chain', which was included along with 'cord' – I did not want to lose the strong image of childbirth associated with that word. 'Key' was not only stronger and more direct than 'symbol' but also gave a full rhyme which made, I felt, a most pleasing sound effect to close the poem.

The second draft had reduced the poem from 43 lines to 32. I put the poem away for a few hours before attempting a third.

Third Draft
Now it was a case of tidying up more than anything else. When I read the poem aloud I was fairly happy with it, and decided to make just a few alterations to produce this version (still with no title):

No clutter covers shelves. Blu tack
scars walls where your stars smiled.
Dust rings mark the carpet; soap
has dried out, cracked; cobwebs cling books.
The room holds just trace scent
of your perfume, and on the floor
one flower.

These petals breathed their part
in first bouquet from first real love.
Blush faded long ago,
aged pink to sepia. Carnation
turned parchment, crisped,
its stem stringed, neck a husked cup.

No accident left this behind
when all the rest were binned.
You moved on, precision placed your link.
Unscented now, your flower
stands in a glass,
flavours the air.

In time to come this room once yours
will change; new furniture and carpets
welcome guests, unlittered by your living here.
Your flower will not belong
and yet
I shall hide it safe behind
stored soap and towels.
An amulet that charmed your growing up
its link tightens our chain,
new cord to bind us,
key to set us free.

Title suggestions:

First flower
Leaving
Unlocked   (preferred)
Amulet   (preferred)
Touchstone

I cut a little of the description and most of the 'yours' from the
first stanza and altered the line structure. I decided that 'one
flower' drew more significance to itself if all the lines which pre-
ceded it were of greater and more or less equal length.

The second stanza lost a couple of non-essential words and was
given a little twist in the grammar of its last two lines.

After the break of a few hours, the line option in the third stanza
had resolved itself, and the eccentric line structure immediately
after it was amended.

In the final stanza I altered the line pattern in order to remove
the comma before 'safe'. I wanted to introduce a hint of ambiguity,

to allow the reader free choice as to whether 'safe' referred to the flower itself or its hiding place. I was unhappy with the phrase 'it closes', and felt that the poem was strengthened when it was dropped.

For the sake of propriety, I shall not reproduce here my comments at the continued lack of a title. Suffice it to say that I resorted to making a list. 'Amulet' was perhaps not the best title, but it was the least worst.

Final Stage

A week passed. I still had no desire to alter the third draft. It was time to send it into the world – the moment when I always want to ask the poem whether its coat is buttoned up, and whether it has a clean handkerchief. In other words, I was sending my baby into the cold.

The 'cold' is tempered for my poems by a most sympathetic first reader, the poet, novelist and broadcaster Peggy Poole. I have the highest respect for her criticism. On this occasion she gained extra Brownie points by telephoning on receipt to say that she enjoyed the poem. She offered her first reactions during the call.

Peggy queried the spelling and possible presence of a hyphen in 'blu tack' – to be checked at the stationer's. (I later discovered that I should have used a hyphen.)

Although I had given no indication of the areas with which I had had problems, she tuned in to the cobwebs and suggested that 'crab' might be a better word than 'cling'. She added that 'trace scent' did not need to be qualified by 'just', and questioned the final stanza. It was interesting to note that the suggestion was to make a stanza break either after 'your living here' or dividing the last four lines from the rest. The initial draft had incorporated her first suggestion.

After further reflection, Peggy returned the manuscript, having added two comments. She was unsure whether the repetition of 'first' in the second stanza was too much or was just right, and felt that 'once yours' at the beginning of the fourth stanza was an overstatement.

The time had arrived for me to make final decisions. I agreed with all of Peggy's comments except one, feeling that 'first bou-

quet from first real love' should be left intact. I decided to break
the last stanza so that the final four lines stood on their own. This
is the result:

Amulet

No clutter covers shelves. Blu-tack
scars walls where your stars smiled.
Dust rings mark the carpet; soap
has dried out, cracked; cobwebs crab books.
The room holds trace scent
of your perfume, and on the floor
one flower.

These petals breathed their part
in first bouquet from first real love.
Blush faded long ago,
aged pink to sepia. Carnation
turned parchment, crisped,
its stem stringed, neck a husked cup.

No accident left this behind
when all the rest were binned.
You moved on, precision placed your link.
Unscented now, your flower
stands in a glass,
flavours the air.

In time to come this room
will change; new furniture and carpets
welcome guests, unlittered by your living here.
Your flower will not belong
and yet
I shall hide it safe behind
stored soap and towels.

An amulet that charmed your growing up
its link tightens our chain,

> new cord to bind us,
> key to set us free.

Set form poem

I find poems in set form a great deal easier to write than those in free verse, so the creative and revision processes are shorter and simpler. The tight frame in which you work exerts a reassuring control, and metrical regularity takes care of the rhythm of your lines.

Initial idea
There was no need for an exercise to prompt ideas in this case. A full line of iambic pentameter presented itself to me, appropriately while I was attending a writers' conference in Scarborough. I glanced out of my bedroom window and realised that the view was identical to that from the hotel a few doors away where I had spent my honeymoon. The line was:

> I wish I could be seeing this with you.

This was an untypically romantic line, as I find it difficult to write love poems; but it had to be a love poem of sorts – and the line had to appear in it at least once.

First draft
I had a feeling from the start that the poem would be fourteen lines long, and would have some of the attributes of a sonnet but would not be a true sonnet. I wanted to start and finish with my line, and possibly repeat it throughout the poem.

Because I was attending talks and discussion groups, it was impossible for me to produce a draft in one sitting. Instead I carried my notebook around with me, and added a few words here and there, aiming to produce a description of that special view interlaced with memories.

By the end of the day I had produced these lines and, as I was creating them so slowly and piecemeal, there were no alterations

to any words within the first draft. The title came quickly and
without conscious thought.

Single Return

I wish I could be seeing this with you –
the way the sun defines the distant cliffs
and tosses cold kaleidoscopes of foam
to tease the gulls. The castle broods. I wish
I could be seeing this with you. The air
bites with familiar taste of salt. Grey road
rings bursts of green to bind the sand. Sharp rocks
intrude to break the drift. I wish I could
be seeing this with you. And memories
surge faster than the sea to draw away
long years – more wonder in remembering
than sunlight bordering this gilded day.
A vision filled with loving spans my view
I wish I could be seeing this with you.

Revision
This, alas, was non-existent. I made the classic mistake of hurling
my poem into the outside world when I reread it a fortnight later
and liked what I saw. I did not even trouble to contact my first
reader.

I have since learned to be very suspicious of a poem I like. It
is usually severely flawed, and my feelings cloud my judgement.

I sent 'Single Return' to a magazine, whose editor was kind
enough to make a few criticisms instead of pointing out that the
world would be a better and happier place if I tore it up instead
of attempting to inflict it on the populace.

Criticism
The editor in question offered three main criticisms. They were
that the poem needed a full set of rhymes; that there were too many
'soft-centred' phrases; and that the penultimate line was 'precious'. He added, however, that he liked the idea of the poem and
wished to see a reworked version.

I found myself in full agreement with the three comments, and added my own criticisms. The poem actually said very little. It did not have a message. It was too loosely formed. Aware of the 'murder your darlings' advice, I still liked the first line and felt it should be repeated.

I had three ideas about the poem. The first was that the form might be wrong, and the close-to-sonnet pattern militated against the effectiveness of the piece. The second was that a little more background should have been included, or a special comment which would make a point strong enough to sustain the whole poem. At the moment it was simply the reflections of one partner returning alone to the site of a honeymoon. An extension of the central thought could be the theme of holding close/letting go within a relationship. This would fit in with the details surrounding the experience. The final thought was that a time scale might be more closely defined.

Second Draft
I decided to attempt the poem in a different form using a rhyme scheme, and thought it would be a good idea to try a terza rima. These lines flowed easily:

Single Return

I wish I could be seeing this with you –
the way the sun defines the cliffs, and wind
whips foam to tease the gulls. Together, two

inseparably one, we felt the spin
of earth beneath our feet compelling us
to move its rhythm, make the dance begin.

We knew the patterns, watched them forge our trust
as tide-turn, day-night spirals stretched to years,
and doubts grew arid, powdered into dust.

The castle broods to parody past fears.
Alone, I do not wither. I am wet

with salt-sprayed seawater, and not with tears.

Here we made promises, and here we set
the course our grafted lives would take. We grew
together strong – each singly stronger – yet

I wish I could be seeing this with you.

As soon as I began to write, this form felt completely comfortable. Any lingering doubts had disappeared by the fourth line. I
felt that the condensed images of the first stanza provided a
stronger picture, and I liked the lingering feel of the enjambement
at the end of the stanza.

The first six lines were heavily larded with definite articles,
but on reflection I decided to keep them. After all, there is no point
in following 'rules' of poetry unless you feel you can break them
from time to time. The same philosophy allowed me to retain the
heavy and overwritten 'tide-turn, day-night spirals' and salt-
sprayed seawater'.

I was happy with the vocabulary, rhyme and metre of the
poem, and felt that this new version conveyed its message; that
the strong bond of marriage makes two people grow as individ-
uals as well as within the confines of being a couple. Not only
was I able to keep my favourite line . . . I managed to use it twice.

Exercises

27 Using any of the 'Finding the Idea' suggestions in Chapter 2,
   start writing a poem in any form as an exercise. Do you reach
   a stage where artistry takes over from the 'mechanical' process?
   If so, can you pinpoint it? If not, do not be alarmed. You are
   thinking about just one example, not a whole range of writing
   from exercises.

28 Return to any poem you have written in a set form and try to
   use its ideas in a different form. Are you pleased with the
   result, or happier with the original version?

29 Start a new page in your notebook for 'found' lines or even complete poems. Write down any words you see or hear in your everyday life which lend themselves to poetry (such as the example prompting the set form poem described in this chapter).

10

PUBLICATION

When you feel you have written the best piece of work you can, there are two possible courses to follow. You could put the poem away in a drawer and forget about it. Or you could attempt to get it published, in order to share the message it communicates with anyone who cares to read it.

There are some poems which are never intended for publication. We write poetry to exorcise our personal ghosts; to express our most primitive reactions in words; to set down feelings we could never air in society. In our youth we write didactic poems aimed at rectifying the ills of the world. All these poems are therapeutic. By writing them we are coming to terms with problems in a way that does not harm ourselves or anyone else. In many cases, these are the poems that should be destroyed or hidden away.

Only a very small proportion of poetry written falls into this category. If you have laboured over your work and sought to produce the best poem you can, it is natural for you to want to see it in print.

Before you attempt to get your poetry published, it is a good idea to consult Peter Finch's book, *How to Publish Your Poetry* (Allison & Busby). The experience he shares through its pages is invaluable.

It is not unheard of for novice writers to bundle up their entire output and send it away to one of the large publishing houses. This leads to the large publishing house returning the entire output. It comes back with a more or less polite note declining the invitation to discover the undiscovered genius. It is far better to send your work away in small batches to the magazines which are at the heart of publishing new poetry.

Little magazines

This is a misnomer. There is nothing 'little' about these publications, except, perhaps, in terms of the number of people operating them. Many such magazines function with a staff of one or two people in sympathy with poetry, and dedicated to bringing the best modern writing to an audience.

There is a wide range of 'little' magazines, covering all forms of presentation from the couple of duplicated sheets stapled together, to the glossy paperback book.

Within their pages appears the most recent contemporary poetry. It may be vital, experimental, traditional, humorous . . . every type of writing is represented.

Some magazines print nothing but poetry, such as *Smoke*, while others such as *Orbis* offer a wide range of features of interest to poets, including editorial comment, correspondence, magazine and competition listings, articles on technique, reviews of poetry books etc.

It is unusual to see these magazines in newsagents or bookshops. Some libraries have them on display, but most people buy them directly by mail order. When you subscribe to one you will hear about others; many magazines carry fliers for other publications and competition entry forms. You will also learn from these (and from magazines devoted to the interests of writers) about anthologies of poetry to which you can submit material.

Editors would, of course, like you to take out a subscription to their magazines. Without readers they could not continue, but a subscription is not a guarantee of acceptance for your work. Nor will your poetry be rejected merely because you are not a subscriber. You would have to have large quantities of money to buy all the magazines available, and time to read them. To be realistic, editors accept that nobody can subscribe to everything. It is in your own interests to read as many as you can. Not only will you be keeping in touch with contemporary poetry, you will be learning something of the special requirements of each editor.

Writers in other fields are urged to seek out a market for their work before they produce it, and tailor their writing to the precise needs of their market. Because there is such a wide range of poetry being published, there are magazines to suit all styles. Although you do not need to take the clinical approach of writing specifically for a market, you should be sure to send your work to a magazine whose content indicates a preference for your style. So the more you study, the more outlets you will find.

Do not expect to make a fortune out of your work. You may be paid a few pounds or in free copies of the magazine. Getting your poetry published is highly satisfying, which is just as well as it is not at all lucrative. Do not give up the day job when your first acceptance arrives.

One of the more enjoyable aspects of submitting poetry lies in getting to know other writers through magazines. Apart from the editor with whom you might build up a rapport, you will recognise names recurring time after time within the pages, and you will learn a little of the other poets' personalities through correspondence pages.

If you are totally unfamiliar with these publications, consult *Small Presses and Little Magazines of the U.K. and Ireland*, published by Oriel, The Friary, Cardiff CF1 4AA.

Preparing poems for submission

However well written your poems may be, remember that they must be presented correctly if they are to merit serious consideration by an editor.

Each poem, however short, should have its own piece of A4 paper. It should be typed in single spacing with wide margins, and your name and address should appear on the sheet. If your poem is a very long one, paperclip two or more sheets together, but type on one side only of each sheet. (Your typed sheet is referred to as a manuscript, or ms.)

Send no more than six poems at a time (some editors specify fewer) with a brief covering letter. The letter should merely offer the poems for consideration. It should not contain any details of your background, writing methods, philosophy of poetry, desire to be published or family life. If an editor wants this sort of information, he will ask for it. Some poets send details or photocopies of their previously published pieces. This is unnecessary, and a practice many editors heartily dislike, preferring to make up their own mind about a batch of poems rather than being shown what other editors thought of a writer's work.

The practice of sending the same poem to more than one editor at a time leads to all sorts of difficulties. As soon as one editor accepts a poem, you have to write to every other to say it is no longer available for consideration. This is a waste of your time and theirs, and could make them bundle up your whole submission and return it to you.

It is far more beneficial to yourself to keep up a steady flow of writing, and to send fresh material to each editor. Then learn patience. Although some editors offer a reply within a month, others will keep you waiting for six months or more. This may seem very unfair, but remember that most editors are squeezing their magazine work into an already tight schedule, and have only a little time each day to deal with their correspondence. Resist the desire to ring or write, and remind yourself how grateful we should be that there are people around who are willing to edit small magazines, offering a forum for new poetry.

Sending a stamped addressed envelope for a reply is a courtesy which should never be ignored. It is also a politeness to wait for a verdict on one batch of poems before you send another to the same editor.

If you are serious about your writing and do not have a typewriter, beg, borrow or buy one. If you can get hold of a word processor so much the better. If you are a poor typist, practise. If your manuscripts are covered with liquid paper stains, get them photocopied so that the marks do not show.

In other words, excuses about the practicalities of presenting neat copies are unacceptable. You had enough faith in yourself to write your poems in the first place. Do not let yourself down by ignoring the conventions of submission, which amount to nothing more than good manners.

Collections

By the time you have had a dozen or so poems published in magazines, you may feel ready to present your work as a collection. Do not be tempted to rush into this. You would not be the first poet to cringe with embarrassment every time anyone mentioned a first collection which represented his total output at the time thrown together in pamphlet form.

Make sure you have a good supply of work with which you are pleased and which has attracted some success. Then follow one of four courses:

1 Find a publisher willing to produce a collection for you. Again you are likely to get a more sympathetic response from a little magazine publisher than you would from a major book-publishing house, or even from one of the larger small press organisations.

Check all the magazines you know to see which also produces collections. If possible, approach an editor who has already used some of your work. Your name will be familiar to him, and he has shown an interest in your poetry.

Send a query letter asking whether he would like to see your collection, and how many poems you should send him.

If he is interested select the appropriate number from your best poems, possibly including some that he has already published in his magazine.

Depending on the editor, there may be a great deal of alteration to be done, or there may be nothing at all. Perhaps the poems you chose will all be included in your book, or you might be asked to submit an entirely different set. You might be asked to rewrite sections of some of the poems. Remember that any opinion of your work must be subjective. Your editor will have preferences which may not coincide with yours. But a sympathetic editor may be willing to discuss your work with you so that a mutually pleasing list of poems emerges. Remember that your name will appear on your collection. If you cannot feel happy with the editor's suggestions and alterations, you might be more content with a different editor.

Perhaps the greatest advantage of this method of publication is that you are not solely responsible for the selling of the book. Nor are you expected to pay towards its costs.

Do not expect to receive much payment. If you are given a number of copies of the book and allowed to buy more at a discount to sell at full price, you are doing well.

2 Find a publisher who likes your work and is willing to produce it on a subsidy basis. Once more you may be dealing with the editors who produce little magazines. In this case you would be sharing the high costs of production, and you might be expected to play a large part in the sale of the books. Your approach should be the same as that described above. Again you are likely to experience editorial criticism and/or help with your collection.

3. Go to a vanity publisher. He is somebody who advertises publishing services, and will print anything you send him in return for your money. (Quite a lot of money. He makes a living from his work.)

   He will praise your poetry to the skies, tell you that you are an undiscovered genius, and that he would love to produce your work . . . but publication expenses being so high, he would expect you to provide all the finance for the venture.

   You would not get the benefit of editorial advice. After all, if you are willing to part with your cash, there is no need for him to take any undue trouble with your work. You would probably have to do the bulk of the marketing yourself, if not take over all the distribution of your books.

   You will see few copies of vanity publications in bookshops or libraries. You will see fewer being reviewed. Appearing in this format is more likely to harm your growing reputation as a poet than advance it. But it is an option. If you are wealthy and desperate to see your work in print, you may think vanity publishing is worthwhile.

4. You might choose to publish your own book. Self-publication is a far cry from the vanity publishing described above, and

has a long and recognised tradition.

You may have complete faith in your work, but find that there are no openings available to you. Perhaps everyone you approach has a full list and is not considering any new titles. Perhaps you simply want full control over the production of your book, choosing your own quality of paper, style of printing and illustrations.

There is nothing to stop you from taking your collection direct to a printer and hiring his services to produce your book. If you decide to do this, talk to more than one printer. Their quotations will vary considerably, and you might be able to cut costs by doing some of the work yourself, for example by providing camera-ready copy if you have a top-quality printer.

There are certain formalities of which you need to be aware if you are producing your own book, such as requesting an ISBN (International Standard Book Number) and providing the required six copies to the copyright libraries. But all this information and everything else you need to know is readily available in another book by Peter Finch, *How to Publish Yourself* (Allison & Busby). Invest in a copy of this before you even contemplate self-publication. Follow its advice step by step, and you cannot go wrong.

There are just two drawbacks to self-publication. One is that you will need to put a little extra work into your book (the work which a publisher would do for you), and attend to all the funding and marketing of your collection. The selling need not be a chore – but if you cringe at the idea of asking your friend, librarian or bookseller to buy a copy, you may find this side of things difficult.

The other problem is that you do not have the benefit of an editor's advice regarding your poetry. To be brutal, you may think your work is better than it really is. You may not have noticed all sorts of tiny flaws in your poetry which could be put right quite easily if only there was someone to point them out to you. Your selections from your total output may have been prejudiced by your preferences rather than chosen with your most critical eye.

You can get around this problem if you wish. There is

nothing to stop you from approaching a poet of your acquaintance whose work you admire – possibly your first reader – and asking that person to act as editor for you. You are asking a lot, as the task of reading, analysing and criticising a collection is an arduous one, but a fellow poet may be prepared to undertake it for the love of poetry. Or you can offer to return the favour at some time in the future.

It is an increasing trend for poets to publish their work in aid of charity, donating the profit on their sales for some good cause. If you do this, make sure that you include only your best work. If the charity is worth helping, it deserves your best. And remember that you should not exert pressure on people to buy your book because of the special connection.

Whichever road to publication you choose, you may be certain that there will always be critics who slate your book in reviews. There will always be friends who praise it. There will always be a cache of unsold copies in your study. But nothing in this world compares with the sense of satisfaction you feel when you hold your own book of poetry in your hand.

Other outlets

Little magazines, anthologies and individual collections are the traditional markets for poetry, but it is a good idea to be aware of the other outlets for your work. By having your poems appear wherever you can, you are not only establishing yourself in people's minds as a poet, but also helping to promote poetry in a variety of different areas.

Have you considered radio? Apart from the well-established poetry programmes on Radio 4 there are potential outlets all over the country in the local radio network.

Approach your local BBC station and ask whether it broadcasts a writing programme, which may include stories and features as well as poetry. If it does, listen to the programme to get some idea of the style of poetry selected. If it does not have such a programme, you might make the suggestion that one could be planned.

Remember that radio allows the listener just one chance to hear your poem. A piece with a highly complex network of images or a verse form that only works when you see it on the page will not be suitable for this medium. Expect to receive a token payment for any work used.

Are you artistic? If so, you might consider presenting your poetry on posters. You could use attractive lettering and print over a background design or make a collage around your poem. Seek out specialist photocopying services to produce copies of such work. See whether local craft shops would be interested in stocking them. Give framed versions away as presents. On a smaller scale, write poems for reproduction on bookmarks.

Create highly individual greetings cards by producing personalised verses to suit the occasion. Start by making cards to celebrate your friends' birthdays or other special events, and the idea could catch on. You will be doing this strictly for the fun of it (at least to begin with), but it is an entertaining pastime for you, a pleasure for the recipients and a way of becoming better known as a poet within your immediate circle.

Have one side of your plain postcards printed with a poem and a simple illustration, dividing the other side in two for the message and address. Again, you are spreading your 'fame' as a poet to everyone with whom you correspond.

Contact your local theatre group to see if they would like to use appropriate pieces of poetry in their programmes. Check your district newspapers. If they do not usually carry poetry, approach them with ideas for pieces based on topical events or places of interest in the locality.

Poetry appears on the London Underground. Why not check out the public areas of your town to see whether poems could be exhibited there?

Apart from the range of little magazines, look at all the special interest papers on newsagents' shelves. There are publications dedicated to every pursuit you can think of, and a few more. Their editors may be willing to publish poetry that comes within the sphere of interest of the magazine. So if you have poems about computers, caravans or countryside tucked away, you may find new outlets within their pages.

Do not forget the market for light verse that exists within the readers' letters pages of women's magazines. These pieces should be simply and directly written, and almost invariably rhyming and metrical. They are quick to write, and provide a moment's relaxation from the more demanding poetry. Keep them short, and do not use overlong lines. (They will be published in narrow columns.) Expect to receive payment of a few pounds for each acceptance.

If you enjoy these light verses, have you thought of trying to write for greetings card manufacturers? Unlike the individual messages mentioned earlier, these should be as impersonal as possible. (E.g. 'A message from me/both of us/all of us' automatically restricts its potential market. 'A message to you' could be from one or any number of senders.) Check the writing yearbooks to see which manufacturers are seeking verses. These too are undemanding and relaxing to write.

Remember that I have offered just a few suggestions for airing your poems. Expand the list to include your own pet projects and help to share your excitement of poetry with all who are prepared to read it.

Getting organised

Not the most interesting part of getting your poetry published, but if you want to send poetry out for consideration you need to undertake just a little administrative work.

Keep records on file cards or simply in an exercise book. Note where and when you send your poems and the verdict on them. If you keep a check on the number of weeks each editor holds your work, you will have a rough guide as to when you can expect a reply to your next submission. (Remember that an editor's workload fluctuates. Do not expect identical delays while waiting to hear about each batch you send.)

By keeping a note of the destination of each set of work you will not make the error of submitting a poem to an editor who has already rejected it, so wasting his time and your postage.

Before you send any poems to magazines you might have the

idea that you would never forget the markets to which you sent your work, or the acceptances and rejections that follow. Be assured that confusion sets in as soon as you post the second set.

Make sure that you keep legible copies of all your poems. Although most editors are meticulously careful with your work, they cannot be held responsible if mss go astray. Never allow your only copy of a poem out of your files.

If you work with a word processor, still produce hard copies of your poetry. A single corrupted disc could wipe out a decade's labour.

Exercises

30 If you have not already done so, make clear copies of all your poems and put them together in a ring binder or similar file. You may store them chronologically or in subject categories, but make sure you know your own way around your filing system.

31 Spend some time reading a selection of little magazines, and then divide your mss into batches (of up to six) to be sent away. Be aware of the differences in style and the lengths of poem preferred by each magazine.

32 Make a list of outlets which might accept your poetry, using the ideas offered in this chapter and any others. Go through your list systematically, sending some work to each.

11

THE WORLD OUTSIDE

The more of your work you see in print, the greater the incentive you have to go on writing. But never forget that your writing appears in isolation. The act of producing poems, sending them out by post, and receiving written replies turns itself into a spiral. If you do not have a first reader or a writers' group to consult about your work, you may be writing in a vacuum. The four sections of this chapter suggest areas of the poetry world which are interesting to explore and will keep your writing from becoming stale.

Compete

There is a long tradition of competition among poets, dating from the time when poetry was respectable, paid employment. The bards would organise contests among themselves to refine their craft and to exclude the incompetent. Although the reasons for competing have changed, the tradition continues. Check in your local library or arts centre, in your poetry or writers' magazines, and you will find details of dozens of competitions. They range in scale from tiny local ones to vast international ones attracting thousands of entries.

Enter a competition with the same hope of success with which you buy a lottery ticket. That way you will not be disappointed. But remember that you do not have to rely on luck to make you a winner. By entering the best poem you can write, you are increasing your chances of success.

Not everyone approves of poets competing, so perhaps it would be interesting to consider some of the good and bad points of the whole business.

Competitions aim to encourage and assist poets. They bring

poetry into the open, heightening public awareness of the craft. They offer poets a deadline with all the discipline that imposes. A win or an honourable mention gives enormous encouragement. Some competitions produce books of the best entries, and so provide another publication outlet. They offer a structure of prizes where even the most modest exceed the payments made for publication. The largest offer instant fame and recognition to the winners – bypassing the traditional route to recognition of regular publication over a number of years.

In addition to this, they enhance the status of the organising society, bringing it publicity and prestige. And many competitions nowadays are run in aid of charities, so good causes benefit from the enterprise.

On the negative side, entering regularly without success may be devastating to an inexperienced writer. An already successful writer may be afraid of losing face if he enters and does not win. As your work is being judged not merely on its merit but against every other entry, only a tiny minority of pieces submitted gains recognition. (When you submit work to an editor he is looking for a relatively high number of excellent poems. An adjudicator seeks to place just three or four competition poems.) Despite the promise of large prizes, the entry fees can add up to a substantial outlay over the months. Entry fees should be regarded as dead money. There is no way you can guarantee the returns from competitions.

It has been suggested that there is a special style of 'competition poem' which may be overcommercial or bland. I believe that this suggestion is an insult to the adjudicator's intelligence. The 'competition poem' merely has to be good.

There is no magic formula for writing a winning poem. If I knew one, I should keep it to myself. But if you like the idea of competing, here are six hints that may be of use.

1   Research the competition. Does it seem to have a regional bias? A poem about that locality my have an advantage. Is it in aid of a charity? You might enter a piece that touches on the concerns of the charity involved.

2   Research the adjudicator. What sort of poetry does he write? What themes run through his work? Does he seem to prefer free verse or set forms? Be careful not to send in an imitation of one of his poems; you are merely reminding yourself of his preferences through this study.

3   Whether writing new work for a specific competition on a set theme or selecting from your previous work, enter a poem that will remain fixed in the adjudicator's mind. Competence is not enough. Every competitor will be sending in his best piece of work. Yours has to be better.

4   Keep to the rules to save your time, effort and money. You cannot expect a competition organiser to take the trouble to correct your entry, nor will a late piece be accepted, however good it might be.

5   Keep a record of all your entries to aid your memory and also to make sure you do not send a poem to an adjudicator who was unmoved by the same piece in a different competition last year. If he did not like it then, do not expect him to have changed his mind now.

6   Send for a copy of the adjudication report and winning entries if the competition organisers make these available. You will be able to start building up a dossier on the tastes of the adjudicator. You will also see what sort of poetry is winning prizes. Does the same name crop up time after time in a list of winners? If so, what does that particular writer have that you lack?

Approach competitions professionally. Be businesslike in your entries. A win does more for the morale than a dozen acceptances.

Communicate

The fact that you are writing poetry means you are already communicating, with yourself as its creator and with anyone who cares to read. But an additional level of communication exists in the spoken word. Hearing a poet read his own work is always interesting. From the poet's point of view, it is just as interesting to read to an audience. You will probably feel ready to try your work this way by the time you have had a dozen or so poems published.

If you have had no experience of speaking in public, be realistic about your own talents and limitations. Practise reading your poems slowly and clearly into a tape recorder, then listen to the recording, or better still, persuade a friend to listen for you.

Check that every word can be heard and that your voice is pleasant to listen to. Have you spoken with variety of pitch or on a monotone? Is the pace lively without being gabbled? Have you used pauses to allow your message time to communicate itself? Is the tone of your voice compatible with the subject matter? (E.g. a gentle tone for a light lyric, a stronger tone to put across a forceful message.) Most importantly, are you making sense of your own writing?

Speak your poetry aloud facing a mirror. Does your facial expression enhance the meaning of the words, or is it deadpan, or contorted in a grimace? Are you gasping for breath half way through a line or able to sustain a fluency in your reading? Do you make movements and gestures while you speak? If so, are they distracting?

At this stage if you feel you would like to offer readings of your work but have doubts about your own performance, consult a teacher of speech and drama who will be able to advise and help you.

When you are happy with your voice work, look carefully at your collection of poetry. Think about preparing a balanced programme of readings, remembering that a touch of humour relaxes and pleases an audience. Look at each poem individually, asking yourself whether it would work if spoken out. Some pieces, such as concrete poems, have little validity when spoken. Certain complex forms may sound confusing. But most poems can bring as much pleasure when heard as they can when read from the page.

Once you have chosen appropriate poems and sorted them into a pleasing, balanced order, practise reading them to yourself whenever you can and working out interesting introductions to them. Decide how much you want to say between readings. Some poets like to offer a lot of poems with virtually no explanation. Others prefer to go into details of the circumstances behind each piece and the process of writing. Adopt a technique which pleases you – the choice is yours.

Put your poetry for readings into a loose leaf or display file so that you do not spend time fumbling through books and papers on the platform. You may feel happier writing out your planned introduction at the top of each sheet, but if you can speak this to the audience rather than reading it, you will create a warmer sense of intimacy with your listeners. It is a good idea to develop a programme which lasts for about an hour, and which you could adapt to fit a shorter or longer time slot.

When you are completely happy with your basic programme and your delivery, let people know of your willingness to speak. Contact local societies who have guest speakers. (Most local newspapers carry reports of talks given to different groups.) Get in touch with your regional Arts Association, libraries and writers' groups.

When you are approached to give a reading, make sure you get as many details as possible about the organisation's requirements. A writers' group may be particularly interested in the way you wrote the poems. A local history group might be more interested in poems which chronicle your childhood in the area. A literary society might wish to know your opinions on using set forms. In other words, gear your programme to the audience who will be listening.

Think about practical considerations. Make sure you know the date, time and location of your reading. If you have a collection of your poetry available, ask whether you might sell copies afterwards.

Expect a realistic fee for your work, and remember to ask for travelling expenses. You may be speaking to a Church group or charitable society, and decide to waive payment. The Poetry Society suggests certain rates of pay but these are not necessarily appropriate for every group you address. If a group asks how much you charge and you feel you are on uncertain ground, say, "I'll be happy to speak for your usual fee'. But be warned – this could be a handshake and a pot plant. As a rough guide, check the hourly rate paid by local authorities to their night school staff. Ask for the equivalent of two-three hours' payment. Do not feel embarrassed about being paid for your readings. Performing to the best of your ability then expecting the due rate for this demanding work is a mark of professionalism.

By reading in public you will increase your fame and, more importantly, make a lot of friends. But the rewards you gain in terms of personal satisfaction and encouragement for your writing will prove to be invaluable.

Circulate

Even if you do not live in an area where there are poetry events you can attend, it is possible to get advice on your work from other writers by circulating your poetry among them. You need an initial contact. You can get to know other poets through the pages of poetry magazines or through general writers' publications. Contact your regional Arts Association and ask whether they can put you in touch with others. Better still, enrol for a poetry seminar or course attended by lots of writers.

Having made contact with people who share your interest, you can exchange letters and poems, offering mutual criticism. You can, of course, speak on the telephone. You can also send cassette tapes as 'talking letters'. You might be able to arrange meetings, distance permitting.

One of my favourite advice links with other poets is the 'folio system'. This consists of a file of poems circulating among a number of writers. Each adds two poems to the file, and the other members make comments on the mss, often disagreeing with their fellows' assessments. When everyone has had a chance to comment, the same two poems make a second 'circuit' so that everyone reads all the opinions, and the writer can add his own observations. These poems are then removed and two more new poems are added.

Eventually, you have as many opinions of your work as there are members in the folio group, and can make further revisions

115

based on the comments made. The more members, the more advice you get, but the longer you have to wait for the file to circulate. If everyone agrees to post the file within a week, you should in theory receive the poems regularly and at a frequency of x weeks, if x is the number of members in the group.

I belong to two folios. In one we all live within thirty miles of each other, and arrange occasional meetings. The other is countrywide, and an exercise book circulates with the poems for personal messages and open letters. Both offer invaluable help. Setting up a folio takes only a little effort and three or four interested poets. Ten would probably be a maximum workable number of members.

Congregate

There is no better antidote for writers' block, poets' depression and multiple rejection than getting together with other people in the same boat. Other writers know how you feel. They share your traumas more than the most sympathetic members of your family possibly could. They can think up the most colourful terms of abuse to level at those editors and adjudicators who see fit to pass over your writing. (Even if the editor is your dearest friend, it is more healthy to level abuse in the privacy of your study than to pull a blanket over your head and whimper in the corner when your work is rejected. Needless to say, you would never dream of repeating the abuse, aloud or on paper. You write back thanking the editor in question for looking at your last submission, and enclose your next.)

If you live in an area which has a writers' class, group or circle, you are fortunate. Seek out the meetings, and give them a try. A class will offer the help of a tutor in addition to criticism from other members. You may get artistic, technical and marketing advice from the same source. It is a good idea to chat with the tutor before you sign on for lessons. Many classes explore all aspects of writing, and may devote only one or two sessions of the academic year to poetry. Some are based on lectures by the tutor. Others are built around comment on the mss produced by the students week by week. You may be permitted to sit in as a guest and watch a class before committing yourself to the full course.

Writers' groups and circles tend to be a little less formal in their structure. They differ widely in style, membership, entrance requirements and frequency of meeting. The group to which I belong (Southport Writers' Circle) meets one night a week in the local library. Members include widely published and comparatively inexperienced writers. Most nights are devoted to a brief exchange of writing news followed by an in-depth analysis of eight to ten mss. We have occasional internal competitions, talks by members on their special subjects, and talks by guest speakers. We organise an annual one-day seminar on different aspects of writing, and an international poetry competition.

Everyone has different expectations of a writers' group, and individual reactions to the help offered. I can only say I should have given up writing years ago without the friendship, advice and encouragement offered to me.

Should you find there is no writing group to suit your requirements nearby, why not start one? A press release to the local paper and posters in the library are certain to attract the attention of fellow poets. Arrange meetings for a small group in each other's homes, and you will not have to find the cost of room hire.

It is a good idea to discuss the aims and conduct of your meetings at the outset. decide whether you will write in the course of each meeting, or discuss mss, read published poetry or share ideas about the craft of writing. Consider the question of the formality of a committee structure, and whether you want to restrict your members to a few writers or try to encourage many others to join.

If you are not interested in attending regular meetings, do keep an eye open for the one-day, weekend and week-long seminars and conferences. As with writers' groups, these differ widely in style. Some consist of series of lectures, others allow you an opportunity to write in a more or less formal situation. I cannot imagine anyone attending such a get-together and failing to benefit from the experience. Check your Arts Association magazine and writers' magazines for details of these events. Book as early as you can, or you may not get a place.

If you want time to write with expert guidance in pleasant

surroundings, consider joining an Arvon Foundation course. This involves living in a house-party setting with a group of fellow writers and two tutors. All aspects of writing are covered at the centres (in Yorkshire, Devon and Scotland), but there are numerous poetry weeks throughout the year which you can select.

Consider the Writers' Summer School, held each August in Derbyshire. All writing genres are included in the programme, and between three and four hundred writers congregate to hear talks, take part in discussion groups, exchange information and, occasionally, write. The talk is incessant. You are sure to make friends. Inspiration lurks at every turn.

These are just two examples of the dozens of events on offer. The more you are able to visit, the greater your opportunity to receive advice and help, and to refine your craft.

Write on

No matter how many courses you attend, books you read, or programmes you watch on television, you have to get on with the business of setting words down on paper. There is no short cut to producing good poetry. You have to practise the craft, to keep the writing muscle working. Even practise is no guarantee against writing a poor poem with no message, dire rhymes and an inbuilt groan factor.

Remember that the production of such work has its own special value. It is all part of the process of gaining experience. The worst piece we ever write teaches us something we can avoid in the next poem.

Write regularly, write frequently, write from your heart. And enjoy it.

USEFUL ADDRESSES

(Please remember to send a stamped addressed envelope when requesting information from any of these sources.)

The Poetry Society hosts a wide range of readings and events in London, and has a quarterly magazine, *Poetry Review*, which is sent to members. It operates a professional critical service and administers the prestigious National Poetry Competition. Contact the Society at 22 Betterton Street, London WC2H 9BU.

Orbis is a publication crammed with good poetry and interesting information. Mike Shields, its editor, organises the annual Rhyme International Competition. Details from 199 The Long Shoot, Nuneaton, Warwickshire CV11 6JQ.

Smoke is a magazine full of good poetry. Its publishers produce a leaflet listing dozens of little magazines (available free of charge when you send a s.a.e.). Contact Dave Ward at The Windows Project, 40 Canning Street, Liverpool L8 7NP.

A magazine with plenty of up-to-date information and features about all forms of writing including poetry is *Writers News*. You will learn of numerous courses and seminars in its pages. The address is Writers News Ltd, P.O. Box 4, Nairn, IV12 4HU.

A writer's magazine which administers a series of circulating folios for different genres including poetry is *Springboard*, edited by Leo Brooks from 30 Orange Hill Road, Prestwich, Manchester M25 5LS

Consult your local college of further/adult education for details of writers' classes in your area.

For details of writers' circles all around the country, consult Jill Dick's excellent directory. Contact her at 'Oldacre', Horderns Park Road, Chapel-en-le-Frith, High Peak SK23 9SY.

Brochures listing the Arvon Foundation courses are available from the Foundation at Lumb Bank, Hebden Bridge, West Yorkshire HX7 6DF or Totleigh Barton, Sheepwash, Beaworthy, Devon EX21 5NS.

Writers' Summer School in Derbyshire, contact Brenda Courtie at The New Vicarage, Parsons Street, Woodford Halse, Daventry, Northants. NN11 3RE. As there is a lot of competition for places, it is a good idea to send your s.a.e. by the beginning of January in the year during which you hope to attend.

Every poet has a favourite book list. This is a shortened version of mine. It is not exhaustive – simply a list of the books to which I refer most frequently. I have resisted the temptation to include the life stories of poets, which always fascinate me, or any book which is currently out of print. (It is worth exploring second-hand bookshops to seek these out.)

The Poet's Manual and Rhyming Dictionary by Frances Stillman, published by Thames & Hudson. The first quarter of the book is full of easy-to-follow advice on the techniques of writing. The rest is devoted to the rhyming dictionary, which is comprehensive and well laid out.

The New Book of Forms (subtitled *A Handbook of Poetics*) by Lewis Turco, published by the University Press of New England. If you enjoy set forms, you will love this. If you do not, it could drive you insane. It is full of advice and bursting with forms and their variations.

The Way to Write Poetry by Michael Baldwin, published by Elm Tree Books. For me, this book captures the thrill of poetry. I cannot glance at its pages without feeling an excitement that prompts me to write.

How to Publish Your Poetry and *How to Publish Yourself* by Peter Finch, published by Allison & Busby. Two no-nonsense volumes packed with practical advice. If I had not read the former, it is unlikely that I should ever have bridged the gap between magazine publication and collections.

The Rattle Bag edited by Seamus Heaney and Ted Hughes, published by Faber & Faber. This is a random anthology into which you can dip at any time and find a gem. I keep it beside me for those inevitable moments when poetry seems too much like hard work. It refreshes the soul.

Any dictionary and thesaurus. The dictionary quite simply contains all the words. By browsing through a dictionary you absorb the excitement of words which drives you to write. (Be careful to avoid overuse of your most recently discovered vocabulary.) I use a pocket-sized thesaurus to prompt me to find the right word. There is too large a selection in the full-sized one, and I lose the thread of my writing while considering all the possibilities.

The latest edition of any little magazine. There is something inherently exciting in reading the most recently published poetry. Again it forces me to write.